brilliant

business writing

brilliant

business writing

How to inspire, engage and persuade
through words

second edition

Neil Taylor

**Prentice Hall
is an imprint of**

Harlow, England • London • New York • Boston • San Francisco • Toronto • Sydney • Singapore • Hong Kong
Tokyo • Seoul • Taipei • New Delhi • Cape Town • Madrid • Mexico City • Amsterdam • Munich • Paris • Milan

PEARSON EDUCATION LIMITED

Edinburgh Gate
Harlow CM20 2JE
Tel: +44 (0)1279 623623
Fax: +44 (0)1279 431059
Website: www.pearsoned.co.uk

First published in Great Britain 2009
Second edition 2011

© Pearson Education Limited 2009, 2011

ISBN: 978-0-273-74458-0

British Library Cataloguing in Publication Data
A CIP catalogue record for this book can be obtained from the British Library

Library of Congress Cataloging in Publication Data
Taylor, Neil.
   Brilliant business writing : how to inspire, engage and persuade
through words / Neil Taylor. -- 2nd ed.
      p. cm.
   ISBN 978-0-273-74458-0 (pbk.)
   1.   Business writing.   I. Title.
   HF5718.3.T397 2011
   651.7'4--dc22

                                                    2010049703

10 9 8 7 6 5 4 3 2 1
15 14 13 12 11

Set by 30
Printed by Henry Ling, Dorchester, Dorset

Contents

About the author

Neil Taylor is creative director of The Writer (thewriter. com), the UK's largest business writing consultancy. He trains people to become more effective writers at places like the BBC, British Airways, Sotheby's, and Breast Cancer Care.

He's written two books: *Search Me*, about the Google brand, and *The Name of the Beast: The perilous process of naming products, companies and brands*. He's got a degree in linguistics and crops up from time to time on the TV and radio talking about words and brands.

He got interested in language when he was exiled from Lancashire to the Home Counties, and realised he didn't speak like everyone else. He's done the same trick in French, which he speaks with an odd Québec accent.

Publisher's acknowledgements

We are grateful to the following for permission to reproduce copyright material:

Extract on page 22 from http://www.plainenglish.co.uk/awards/golden-bull-awards/golden-bull-winners-2007.html, © Plain English Campaign; Extract on page 59 from 'Actor says sorry to Cage for false dog claim', *The Guardian*, 5 April 2008 (Gillan, A.), Copyright Guardian News & Media Ltd 2008; Extract on page 133 from *Nineteen Eighty Four* by George Orwell (Copyright © George Orwell, 1949) by permission of Bill Hamilton as the Literary Executor of the Estate of the Late Sonia Brownell Orwell and Secker & Warburg Ltd, also *NINETEEN EIGHTY-FOUR* copyright 1949 by Harcourt, Inc. and renewed 1977 by Sonia Brownell Orwell, reprinted by permission of the publisher; Extract on page 133 from *The Da Vinci Code* (2004) by Dan Brown, published by Bantam Press. Reprinted by permission of The Random House Group; Extract on page 136 from *2002 Ericsson Annual Report* (Ericsson); Extract on page 165 from www.innocentdrinks.co.uk/us/?Page=our_story, © Innocent; Extract on page 176 adapted from www.pauljennings.com.au, by Paul Jennings; Extract on page 192 from 'To cut a long story short', *The Guardian*, 24 March 2007 (Six-word stories by Kate Atkinson, Jim Crace, Helen Fielding, DBC Pierre and George Saunders) Copyright Guardian News & Media Ltd 2008; Lyric on page 198 from *I'm Lucky*, Joan Armatrading, Words & Music by Joan Armatrading © copyright 1981 Imagem Music. All rights in Germany administered by Ronder Musikverlag

GmbH. All rights reserved. International copyright secured. Used by permission of Music Sales Limited, Lyric on page 198 from *Love and Affection*, Joan Armatrading, Words & Music by Joan Armatrading © 1976 Imagem Music. All rights in Germany administered by Ronder Musikverlag GmbH. All rights reserved. International copyright secured. Used by permission of Music Sales Limited.

In some instances we have been unable to trace the owners of copyright material, and we would appreciate any information that would enable us to do so.

Author's acknowledgements

I thank you

My mum and dad, Hazel and Michael, for moving down south when I was five, leaving me with a funny accent and a lifelong love of language.

Martin Hennessey, John Simmons and the good people of The Writer for giving me the chance to do this job I love, and inspiring me with their talents, too.

And Oisín, for again putting up with endless talk of deadlines and word counts.

PART 1

The beginning

CHAPTER 1

Introduction

Or as a journalist would say: tell them what you're going to tell them

Are you a writer? Nearly every week there's an ad like that at the front of the national newspapers, tempting people to give up their lucratively paid jobs in field operations, and instead write the romantic novel they know they've always had in them. And there must be enough of us who are tempted, because this ad runs and runs, and someone, somewhere, is making tons and tons of money every week from people with that dream.

Sound like you? Even if it does, very few of us think of ourselves as a *writer*, and even fewer make a living from it. Yet at work, most of us write. Maybe not 80,000 words of heaving bosoms, but we write stuff – the stuff that helps us do our jobs: e-mails, letters, reports, presentations, websites, brochures, press releases, text messages. There are tons of things that we all produce every day, and it's all written down.

Which is why it's odd that most of us never get any help with it in our careers. You learn to speak, you're taught how to write at school (though not much about how it actually works), you get a job, and that's it. For most of us, for the next forty years, you're on your own.

Well, that's fine, you might be thinking. I can write. I wouldn't have got my job if I couldn't. I put my CV together, and rattled off my covering letter, so they knew I could write, right? Well, maybe. We can all breathe, but most of us don't know the techniques that help you breathe well enough to be a brilliant singer. Most of us can dance a bit, but we're a long way off brilliant dancers like Michael Jackson. Heck, most of us can talk, yet big businesses spend millions every year on training people to become better presenters, because we've all seen the difference between someone who can just about stand up and speak without falling over or spitting on the front row, and someone who makes a truly brilliant best man's speech.

So why should we settle for writing that's just OK? We shouldn't. That's what this book is about. Having the confidence and creativity to take your business writing from something that does the job into something that's brilliant; something that does the job better: wins you more work, convinces more people, or gets you the promotion. Because brilliant business writing will help you do all of these things. So it's for you. Of course it's for you if you call yourself a business writer (although if you do, you're probably using these techniques fairly instinctively). Yes, it's for you if you've got anything like 'communications' in your job title. But it's also for you if you just write as part of your job. And there can't be many of us these days who don't.

What do I know about it? Well, it's what I spend my time doing. I'm creative director of a company called The Writer, based just round the corner from Borough Market on London's South Bank, and we help people turn their business writing from boring to brilliant (we hope). And we train them how to do it. So this book is the fruit of many years writing, helping others to write, and helping their organisations (and ours) do better, make money, or do whatever it is they've got to do.

Will it transform the way you write overnight? I'd like to think so, but maybe not. Think of it like circuit training: you'll be gradually building up your linguistic muscle. It will be hard work in the beginning to change the way you write, because some people have spent their entire careers writing in the same way. It takes time and effort to change those ingrained habits. But with a bit of practice, it can become second nature – partly because some of the techniques are about writing as you would really speak, if you

> think of it like circuit training: you'll be gradually building up your linguistic muscle

weren't trying so hard to sound clever and professional. And partly because writing like this should be more interesting. I firmly believe that more engaging writing is more effective writing, and to make your writing more engaging you have to be engaged in it as you're writing it. That's what this book will be about.

The rule is there are no rules (sort of)

Writing is also tricky because while I'll be giving you guidance, there are no really hard and fast rules. The beauty of language is that there are things that you will write that have never ever been written before; with a finite set of words and constructions, there is an infinite set of possibilities. So I can't say *always* use this word, and *never* use this one. It's not like

> there are no really hard and fast rules

design, where people set rules all the time; they say 'the logo must always appear in these colours and in this amount of white space'. For every word of every sentence you'll have to exercise your judgement about what is clearest, most natural, or most interesting, depending on the effect you're trying to create.

Clearest,

most natural,

or most interesting.

Those are three ideas that are going to come up again and again, because in a way, they are steps on a journey to the perfect bit of business writing. And they're the starting point for the main sections of this book.

First, how do you make what you're writing **clear**? Sure, that's about the words you use, but before you even start writing, you need to think about what you've got to say, the order that you're going to say it in, and how you're going to lead your (sometimes unwilling) reader through it. That's **structure**, and appropriately enough, that's what we'll be starting with.

Once your thought process is sorted out, and easy to follow, you need to make sure your words are just as easy. And usually, that's about making your writing as **natural** as possible, so that your reader takes in what you've got to say with as little effort as possible. So the second section is about getting the **style** of your writing right.

But a bit of writing might be well structured, and feel really natural – utterly competent, in fact – but still not make a massive impact. So with the first two in place, you can then make your writing **interesting**, if it's not quite there already. So Part Four is about the little bits of **magic** that make the difference between a good bit of business writing and a brilliant one.

That's what we're going to cover. First, though, there are a few big things we need to think about or clear up, themes which are going to keep rearing their ugly heads unless we talk about them now. So it's time to get a few things straight.

What is business writing?

Well, to me, it's pretty much any bit of writing that people do at work, except journalism or creative writing. What separates business writing from these other two is that with business writing, the writing isn't an end itself; you're writing to help you (or your organisation) do something else. Mind you, that something else could still be incredibly varied. It could be:

- letters to customers to sell more stuff
- proposals to companies to get work out of them
- reports to the board to tell them what you're up to
- e-mails to colleagues to get them to help you with your workload
- websites to tell the world who you are.

All kinds of stuff. And that means business writing isn't restricted to what we think of as businesses. It could also include charities, individuals, government departments. In fact 'work writing' might be a better description.

Clearly then, business writing comes in all shapes and sizes. There are lots of different reasons for writing, lots of different types of reader, and lots of different formats. But luckily for this book, the same principles apply to many of these, because you've got the same challenges. In fact, as we go on, the most significant distinction will probably be in the length of the documents you're writing. But even then, it only really comes down to two main types: short and long.

Short types of writing:

- e-mails
- most letters
- most internet and intranet articles
- ads
- telegrams from the Queen (well, it's someone's job to write them).

Long types of writing:

- annual reports
- proposals
- white papers
- speeches
- business books.

Of course, there aren't hard and fast rules about what falls into which category. There are some e-mails (usually the bad ones) which are really long, and some proposals (usually the good ones) which are really short. But most of the time, it'll be a helpful distinction. For the sake of argument, let's say that short writing is anything less than 500 words long, and long writing anything over 500 words.

Why should you trust me?

I've been writing most of the different types of documents on the list above for over ten years. And for the last eight, I've spent most of my time training other people how to do it. I've worked with different sorts of organisation, different levels of people with different education, and with different industries, all using different types of writing.

What's interesting is that their strengths and weaknesses are pretty similar. One day, not long ago, I ran a training session in the morning at BBC Radio 1, training the people who write the website for DJs like Chris Moyles. Then, in the afternoon, I was at the revered auction house Sotheby's, helping them write proposals. Now, even though these places are only about five minutes' walk away from each other in London's West End, in spirit, they're a million miles apart. At Radio 1 – trainers, jeans, artfully gelled hair and studied cool. At Sotheby's – wood panelling and nicely cut grey suits. Yet when we talked about what they liked and disliked in business writing, they said nigh on exactly the same things, almost word for word. Which says that when it comes to this subject, and whoever you're writing for, there are some universal truths. Things that you can add to your writing, and things you can cut out of the way you write at the moment, which will bring your writing to life.

So, what you'll get in this book are all the tips and techniques I've spotted, invented and borrowed (OK, OK, stolen) to help people make their writing more effective.

What will it do for you?

You've splashed out on this book, so you want it to help you. I'd like to promise that if you follow what it says, fame and fortune will be yours. I'd like to, but I can't. But it will get you on the right road. Early on in my working life, someone said to me 'people with good communications skills always over-perform in their careers'. What he meant was that if you took two people with exactly the same practical skills, experience and knowledge, the one who was better able to present his or her ideas – either in writing or in person – always did better (much to the chagrin of the other, embittered one). And it's true. If you look at the most successful business leaders, or the most trusted political leaders, they tend to be the best communicators. They get their ideas across quickly, clearly and memorably. If you get to the end of this book and you can do the same thing, you'll do better at whatever career you've chosen than before you started.

And what does that mean? Well that depends what you do. It might mean you sell more beer, or get more money in for your charity. You communicate your policy better, or get your team to like you more. Whatever it is you need to do, it'll help you do it better.

But there are two other sneaky benefits, too. With a bit of practice, it'll help you write faster. Cut down the time you spend writing, and there'll be more time for watching *Doctor Who*, listening to Belle & Sebastian records, travelling to Scandinavia, or whatever it is you want to do with your time (those three are what I'll be doing when I've finished this book, by the way).

But the second one is a little less tangible. Get this writing stuff right, and it'll make you happier. Maybe not in a kind of jumping-for-joy-and-kissing-the-ground-on-your-way-into-the-office kind of way, but a wee bit happier.

> be more yourself, and you'll get better at your job

Why? Because the best business writing works because it puts across something of the author's personality. That means: be more yourself, and you'll get better at your job. That's why my colleague John Simmons often advises people, 'bring your personality to work'. It works. And if avoiding becoming a dreary corporate automaton can help you get further in your career, then that can only be a good thing.

I've said that this book is going to be full of tips and techniques, and I wasn't lying. But not just that. It'll work even better if, before you start even attempting any of these tricks, you 'get your head in the right place', as all the dodgiest football managers would say. So, before we get going proper, there are a few important principles to bear in mind.

1. Be pessimistic about your readers

Why? Because they're just like you (and me). One of the things I'll keep rattling on about in this book is what you can learn from other writing disciplines – poetry, fiction, rhetoric, and so on – and how you can apply that to your own writing and improve it. But there is one thing that you can't borrow from these other, traditionally more interesting forms of writing, and that's your reader's attitude.

Let's face it. If they've spent £9.99 on a novel or, even more economically, taken one out of the library, they're probably feeling fairly generous towards its writing; or, if not generous, at least open. They're unlikely to read the first page – let alone the first line – of the latest Alexander McCall Smith and decide that, if it's not quite floating their boat, it's not worth persevering with. Heck, even the harshest of readers will give most books a chapter to get into their stride.

That is most definitely not the case with business writing. Because we are bombarded and battered with tons of text. We're drowning in great gushing torrents of corporatespeak. Which means that our readers – because they're just like us – are pretty ruthless judges. If our first page is a bit heavy going, or if the first paragraph feels a tad waffly, or if the subject line of our e-mail seems boring, what do they do? Something else. Anything else: make another cup of tea, fill in their timesheet, or switch on for five minutes of Jeremy Kyle (that's for those of my lucky readers who claim they're working from home as they read this – we all know what you're up to).

So the first thing you need to come to terms with is that, even as a brilliant business writer, your readers don't want to read what you've written. They're only reading it because they have to. They will never take your board report to read on the beach in Fuengirola. So, you've got two choices as a writer. Either, you make it really easy to skim-read what you've written, so that they can get the maximum out of it in the minimum time. The secret to that is all in structure and sub-heading, which we'll come to in the next chapter. Or, you make your writing so entertaining that, against their better judgement, and despite the fact that really they should be packing their bag for a fact-finding trip to a food-packing facility in Nuneaton, they just can't help but read it. That's harder, but Parts Three and Four will give you a leg-up.

But blethering on and banking on the fact that your reader will press on just because your document is something they *should* read is never going to work. More likely is that they won't read all of what you've written. Or, on a bad day, any of it. That's why you should do your damnedest to make everything you write interesting; and if you really can't do that, you need to make it at the very least easy to deal with. If it's difficult to read *and* dull, your writing is damned.

Of course, this is gutting if you're the writer. If you're writing up a project that you've been working on, your instinct is to take the reader through every last thing you've done. You want your reader to know everything you've been up to for the last six months. It's a little bit dispiriting to think they simply don't care. But they really don't. And you're writing

you're writing for your reader, not for you

for your reader, not for you. It's about what they're interested in, not what you've got to say.

2. Be optimistic about your readers

I know, I know, that flatly contradicts the previous point. But that's just a cheap writerly trick to keep you reading. There is a point here, though. Yes, your reader is less interested in what you're writing than you are. But remember, they're just like you. It means you know exactly what to do to make your writing work for them.

Over the rest of this book, we'll talk about how to do the things that people consistently say they like in a bit of writing, and not do the things they don't (this is a result of years of research in my training workshops). Things like (on the good side):

- getting to the point
- telling stories
- a clear point of view
- unusual vocabulary.

And (on the bad side):

- not getting to the point
- jargon
- the most important thing coming too late
- unnecessary exclamation marks (!!!)
- (and tons more).

As I've said, this kind of feedback is remarkably consistent. Everyone, but everyone, says the same thing. But something else is remarkably consistent. Yes, people say, *I* like these things in a bit of writing; but I do have this audience who expect something different. Who that audience is depends on who we're talking to; all of these have been accused, in my workshop, of wanting writing which is more formal, technical, or dense: lawyers, investors, MPs, managers, government departments, medical professionals, curators, people who work in the NHS and astronauts (OK, I made that one up).

Interestingly, when those people themselves come to the training (though I've never asked any astronauts), they say the same thing – 'I like this stuff, but this other audience don't.' It's nonsense. I've never met this mysterious group of people who want things to be long, boring and complicated, yet everyone tells me they exist. Well, they don't.

What are you scared of?

So what's really going on here? What's going on is we're all scared. We're scared of what people think of us. We all spend our lives judging and being judged. And writing feels like very documentary evidence for people to judge us on. We don't want to make basic mistakes like spelling a word wrong, or getting an apostrophe in the wrong place. But we don't just want to make sure people don't think we're thick; we actively want them to think that we're clever. So people use impressive-sounding words and formal constructions so that they look intelligent or what people sometimes describe, very vaguely, as sounding *professional*. When I ask people in workshops what their favourite words are, they often even volunteer words that they like to use because other people don't understand them. A man the other day said, 'I like the word *ameliorate*. It means the same as *improve* but you put it into a bit of your writing and everyone has to look it up.' How did he know you have to look it up? Well, he admitted the first time he heard it *he* had to look it up. Now, I love language – that's why I do the job that I do – and I'm all for people expanding their vocabulary. But if you're using words because you know other people aren't going to understand them, I'd say something was going a bit wrong. It's making yourself feel clever by making other people feel stupid. And if professional means what I think it does – doing the best job you possibly can – then that isn't *professional*, because you're not communicating as clearly and straightforwardly as you could.

And writing is also scary because it's exposing. Just like the way we speak, it can reveal things about our backgrounds, our upbringings, our attitudes, our understanding and our talents. Twice in my eight years of training people to write, I've had people leave a workshop very early on in floods of tears – not because of my brutal approach, or sadistic exercises, you understand. But because, in both cases, these people (and one of them was *extremely* senior in their organisation) had been told by particularly unhelpful teachers way back when that they just couldn't write. And that embarrassment had stuck with them through years and years of education and working life. The fact is they *could* write. They probably weren't going to win the next Pulitzer Prize but, given a chance, they were perfectly capable of expressing themselves clearly and confidently.

Madness. Everyone is trying to impress everyone else. Most of us, on some level, are insecure wee people. But I'd say there are much more significant things to be insecure about than writing. Most of us are pretty good writers if we let ourselves be. So, remember, your reader is just like you. They might

> there's no need to show off, or try to impress

be you with twenty years' more experience, or you in a different job, but they're close enough. There's no need to show off, or try to impress. 'Do as you would be done by.' Write to them the way you'd want them to write to you.

3. Business writing is changing

I spend a lot of my time in training sessions persuading people that the way they write for business needs to change. They, unsurprisingly, and not unreasonably, often ask why. After all, some people have been writing in the same way for forty years – probably the way they were taught at school, or university, or secretarial college – and have always done perfectly well with it, thank you very much. And that's true, they have. Their writing has got the job done. But could it get the job done better? More engagingly? With more of their personalities coming over? Very probably.

And it needs to, because what we think of as business writing is changing. Fifteen years ago, business writing usually took place in a printed medium – a letter, a brochure, things like that – and these forms of writing, especially the *official* letter, are very conservative. Business writing originally evolved from legal language, and we know how precise and complex and deathly dull legal language is to read. As a result, fifteen years ago commentators were bemoaning the fact that we lived in an increasingly visual culture, with children weaned on telly, films, video games, even music delivered primarily through visual channels. Children, they said, didn't want to read and, soon, wouldn't need to write.

The return of the word

But then look what happened. The internet arrived, and transformed the way we communicate, and reintroduced the written word as a significant aspect of our lives – our working lives in particular. Now we research and buy things online, we negotiate over e-mail, we express our opinions on blogs, and we keep in touch with our friends using text messages and tweets. Most people probably spend much more time writing at work than they would ever have done those fifteen years ago. Words are back.

> the internet arrived, and transformed the way we communicate

But they're not the same sort of words. The language of mobiles, and e-mails, and blogs, and even the most corporate of corporate websites, is not like that of formal written letters. Because these media evolved in different ways – being shorter, and expecting much more input from and maybe even interaction with the reader – the language evolved, too. The language in all of these media varies a little, actually, but they're all quite a long way away from what we'd been used to up to then. Because of the expectation of brevity and the ease of getting interaction with or response from your reader, the style of this language is much more everyday and conversational; after all, that's the sort of language we're used to using when we want to interact with someone in real life.

So what does that mean for business writing? Well, if we're seeing more writing at work than ever before, and that language is more conversational and less formal than ever before, it means our expectations have changed. A letter that would have been fairly typical fifteen years ago was probably fairly formal. But that would've been no surprise because it would've been adopting the tone of most of the business writing you'd have seen every day. Our reactions, I'd suggest, even if they're fairly subconscious, would have been fairly neutral to a bit of writing like that.

These days, if we got the same letter, in the same tone, it probably wouldn't feel quite the same. Because by the time you receive that letter, you've probably already read an e-mail or a free paper on your way to work, had a look at your favourite website, or whatever. So that letter is not going to feel like it's taking the run-of-the-mill tone of most bits of business writing. It's going to seem much more serious, and much more formal, because it's avoiding the language of everyday conversation that we see most of the time. In fact, it might even seem like it's deliberately trying to sound officious, or stand-offish. In short, what used to seem neutral now seems quite formal. Now, your reader might not consciously pick up on that, but they're probably dimly aware of it somewhere. And in that dim somewhere, they might be thinking: Why are they talking to me like that? Why are they so up themselves? Who do they think they are? Or something like that. Your letter might have got their back up before you've even started; not because of what you've said, just because of the way you've said it.

I think business writers need to recognise that. So even if you have been successfully writing for your entire career, if you want to keep persuading people, if you want to keep them on side, now might be the time to change the way you write. Not 2 strt wrtng in txtspk, but to remove the extremes of formality that aren't going to be doing you any favours.

4. Write more like you speak

Really, this is a question of style. But it's so important that it will colour nearly everything we do in this book. The main way for most of us to become better business writers is to write more like we speak.

Sounds simple, doesn't it? And maybe, sounds wrong, too. After all, many English teachers used to spend much of their careers trying to persuade their impressionable young charges that they had horrible common manners and ways of speaking, and if they could only get their writing a bit posher they'd be able to finally drag themselves up by their bootstraps out of the gutter and into polite society. But the fact is, most of us are good at talking. That's why we're called native speakers; it just comes naturally. We started speaking long before we could write, and some have argued that speech is the one big evolutionary advantage we had over other animals (the ones that share 97 per cent of our DNA). Speaking got us where we are today.

Yet, somehow the impression still abounds that writing is somehow 'better' than speaking – that speech is lazy, corrupt, second class. Well, it ain't. There are differences, but they're just two different systems for doing the same thing: getting your point across.

But most of us are more engaging in person than we are on the page (apart from the odd miserable writer, writing down for posterity all the things he wished he'd said). We explain things quickly, clearly, straightforwardly, naturally and, most importantly, with personality. Yet, I've seen brilliant speakers who somehow seem to swap heads, Worzel Gummidge-style, when they start to write. They become dry, corporate and predictable. And for those reasons, their writing just isn't as effective as they are in person. So,

> most of us are more engaging in person than we are on the page

much of this book will look at tuning in to the way we speak, and trying to get some of that flavour into the way we write.

And I do mean some of that flavour, not all of it. I'm not suggesting we all write literally as we speak. If we really did that properly, it could mean each of us spelling things differently to match our accents, writing in the 'innit's and 'wotcha's and everything else – things that you get the chance to explain in person that you wouldn't on the page. I once gave a presentation at RNID, the charity for people who are deaf or hard of hearing. While I talked, a stenographer typed up what I said, and it appeared on a screen at the side of the stage. In one of the breaks, I sneaked round to have a look, and it appeared like complete gibberish. Sentences begun and never really, well, you know... Starting with one thought, and actually let me say first that... It was all over the place. We're adept at following this stuff in person, with lots of visual clues to help explain what's going on, but on the page? It looked a mess.

The beauty of writing is the fact that you get the chance to hone it, craft it, until it's perfect. The trick is to hone it while keeping it real – holding onto the quality of a real person talking, while making it straightforward and unambiguous. A good test is: would you be able to say it if you were stood in front of a room full of people? In that situation, our words have to be on their best behaviour, but we still want to come across like a real person. If you can imagine yourself saying it, it will sound natural when your reader reads it in their head. If you can't or you wouldn't, you need to refine it until it works.

5. More than just plain

A lot of people associate the kind of business writing I'm advocating with plain English. It's a well-known concept, partly because of the Plain English Campaign. They run awards every

December highlighting the worst excesses of corporate gobble-dygook. A recent winner was Virgin Trains, for this priceless bit of nonsense about ticket pricing structure:

> *Moving forwards, we as Virgin Trains are looking to take own-ership of the flow in question to apply our pricing structure, thus resulting in this journey search appearing in the new category-matrix format. The pricing of this particular flow is an issue going back to 1996 and it is not something that we can change until 2008 at the earliest. I hope this makes the situation clear.*

Awful, I agree. And it's true that, in some areas, what I pro-pose will overlap with plain English. But some people see plain English as dumbing down. Writing everything in a plain way, they argue, is pandering to the lowest common denominator. It makes our writing childish and patronising.

So here's where I agree and disagree. I don't think writing things in a simple way needs to make your writing childish; after all, there is a difference between something which is simple and something which is simplistic. What's so brilliant about the best business writers is the knack they have of taking something that's complicated and making it feel really straightforward. And as a writer, I think I have the confidence not to have to use unnecessarily long or complicated words to impress my reader into thinking that I know what I'm talking about. Hopefully the quality of my thinking will do that. There are reams of corporate writing which, to me, feel dumbed up. They're trying so hard to sound smart that it ends up puffed-up and ridiculous. And naturally, there are cer-tain situations when I just don't want to have to wade through overly complex language; the instructions to the fire exit in an airport, for example. There's no need for that to be written in a way that is anything other than plain.

> there is a difference between something which is simple and something which is simplistic

On the other hand, if you read things that have got the Plain English seal of approval, while they might be clear, they can also be dull as ditchwater. Apart from the most functional situations, plain English can tend to drain the personality out of things. And clearly, if we're trying to get our readers interested in what we're writing, that's not going to do the trick, either. If I met you at a business meeting, and when I got back to the office one of my colleagues asked me, 'What was she like?' and I replied, 'Yeah, fine, she was plain,' you'd be pretty insulted. And no surprise there, because as The Writer's managing director Martin Hennessey once wrote in the *Financial Times:*

Who wants to be plain in life? No professional writer I know.

So what we're faced with, then, is a spectrum. Typical business writing has a personality, but it's not a particularly likable personality: it's formal, stiff, cold and authoritarian. So plain English is good if it can neutralise the worst aspects of that negative persona and, just as importantly, make the writing clearer and quicker to read. But it's only the first step along the personality spectrum; once you've got your writing to be plain, next you need to do something else. You need to inject a more interesting personality, and you can do that in all sorts of ways. You might do that through stories, rhythm, metaphor, or many other techniques which we'll come to later. But you might also do it through words – choosing words which are more unusual, more interesting, more resonant, or whatever.

And that's always my response to people who accuse me of dumbing things down. Yes, I recommend getting rid of language which is wilfully complicated, obscure or formal. But I don't advocate replacing that with words of one syllable which a five-year-old child has to be able to understand. Instead, I say replace the default formal vocabulary with words that are familiar, but lively. There is a cliché that the people who write for the *Sun* are the best journalists in the UK. It's not necessarily true, but to write for the *Sun* you do have to have that knack of translating often dry, boring stuff into language which is both accessible and really engaging. While you might not like the *Sun*'s attitude, and – understandably – you might not want to write your business letters in the same tone of voice, you have to admire their ability not to let anything be boring. And they do that pretty much every day.

6. The two grammars

For the record, neither is this a book about grammar, spelling or punctuation. Why? Well, first, there are gazillion books on those subjects, and no need for me to add to the unfortunate forests of paper devoted to them. So if you want to know about that stuff, read one of them. Second, because, as a business writer you don't always have to slavishly follow the rules of grammar. Sometimes – shock, horror – your writing is better when you don't.

Now, of course, as soon as I write these words, there are language sticklers ready to jump down my throat and berate me for joining the hordes of ill-educated oafs (or should that be oaves?) slowly chipping away at the once solid fabric of the great English language. You know who you are. And my first response to those people would be that I'm not uneducated; I've got a degree in linguistics from Cambridge, thank you very much. And it's to linguistics we must turn to help us suss out what we think about all these grammatical rules.

Really, there are two grammars. There's the one you were taught at school, which is basically a set of (fairly arbitrary) linguistic rules you just have to learn (typically things like not splitting an infinitive, or not writing *can't* or *won't*). And there's what linguists call grammar. Linguistics people also define grammar as a set of rules, but not a set of rules you have to learn consciously, as long as you're a native speaker of the language. You pick these rules up as a child, and we're not completely sure how; probably a mixture of imitation, trial and error and maybe a bit of hard-wiring in the brain, too. These rules are less about what's right and what's wrong, and more about what makes sense or what sounds natural in any language. And when I say 'language', I mean any version of that language.

Take a standard English sentence like 'We did that yesterday.' A speaker of London English might say in casual speech, 'I done that yesterday.' The grammar you learnt at school says it's wrong, but a linguist would say it's non-standard; not wrong, just different. Millions of people say it every day and to the people they're talking to, it sounds natural and makes sense. On the other hand, a sentence like 'Did we yesterday it' doesn't make any sense. So a linguist would say that's ungrammatical in English (and linguists use an asterisk before a sentence to show it's an 'impossible' sentence).

As a business writer, you have to tippy-toe between these grammatical extremes. You will have some very fuddy-duddy readers whose heart rate will mildly increase if they see the word *but* at the beginning of a sentence. But it *is* perfectly natural, and it makes sense, and sometimes it's going to give you the right effect. I'm not saying you should put apostrophes in the wrong place or split infinitives for the hell of it (just as I would probably never write 'We done it yesterday', unless I was really trying hard to reflect the flavour of actual speech), but you need to be willing to question some of the nonsense you were taught at school, if it makes your writing easier to read, or more interesting, or more engaging. To help challenge some of this guff, there's a healthy mythbusting section coming up later on.

7. I fought the law

Another big problem with business writing is that you're not always writing about your own subject or using your own material. Often, you'll have been supplied with content from another source. Rather than writing about your own ideas, in your own way, you might find yourself trying to translate someone else's.

This happens in all sorts of ways in different places that I've worked with. If you're a communicator at, say, Standard Life, you might find yourself trying to make sense of information provided for you by a deeply mathematical pensions expert. If you're writing proposals at Sotheby's, you might be trying to incorporate the thoughts of experts in particular areas of art history. Or the one I come across most often is people dealing with what lawyers have dictated. Because businesses are increasingly terrified of being sued for millions, lawyers in most organisations are having more and more influence, not to say wielding more power. They can shape the way HR policies are written, or what companies marketing themselves can say, or to what extent people will apologise when something goes wrong.

Now, I know these experts are doing a very valuable job. Many of these organisations just couldn't function without them. Yet, when I'm dealing with people who have to write as part of their jobs, lawyers are often singled out for holding people's writing back, restricting it to the formal language that they were educated in. And that's a problem.

When I'm in that situation, I have a simple argument. If I'm producing a bit of writing (even if it's on behalf of one of these people, who might, in real life, be my client, or your boss), then my ultimate responsibility is to my reader. Success or failure is defined by whether they read and understand what I'm writing. To do that, when it comes to the *content*, I will nearly always bow down to the superior wisdom of the expert (usually the lawyer). They know stuff that I don't; that's why they've got their job and I haven't. Where I won't roll over, though, is on the language used to express that content. After all, that's what I know about. That's why I've got *my* job, and they haven't. So I will say whatever they want me to say, but not necessarily how they want me to say it.

Sometimes, this is difficult for these experts to accept. The law, in particular, is a very linguistic profession. Cases succeed or fail on the nuances and interpretations of individual words. But while lawyers can be extremely skilful with words, their main focus is writing for other lawyers. Things which seem clear and unambiguous to them can seem like gibberish to me or any other relatively normal reader (look at the terms and conditions of any financial product, and you'll see what I mean). So as a writer, when you find yourself in this stand-off, you need to embrace your status as a skilful communicator. Then this tussle over words can become more of a negotiation, rather than us bending to the will of a senior, highly paid expert.

Some experts – the good ones – get this already. Some of them *are* fantastic writers for the likes of you and me. But for the ones that aren't, you might need some tricks up your sleeve to help them see something of the error of their ways when they're judging your writing.

 **brilliant** action

(a) **Ask for feedback split in terms of content and tone**. If people have the right to comment on or edit your work, you could ask for their feedback to be divided up: which things are they objecting to on content grounds (i.e. it's factually wrong, we're not allowed to say that, or whatever), and which are about the tone of it? The reasonable ones will realise that the second is much more subjective than the first, and that they shouldn't automatically get their way on matters of tone. And for the unreasonable ones... well, in the nicest possible way, you might just have to tell them the same thing. ▶

(b) **Get traffic light feedback**. This is a variation on the above. Get them to mark in red anything they cannot let out the door, and ask for their reasons (not surprisingly, these will usually be content questions). Get them to mark in orange (amber, if your pen or computer can be so accurate), anything that they'd rather not see written down, but wouldn't actually cause them any tangible problems. Again, this is a way of subtly hinting that anything amber is much more subjective, and gives you leeway to ignore their comments if you don't agree with them.

(c) **Do two versions**. If you're really struggling, do two versions that *mean* exactly the same thing, but have different tones. If you've done a good job, there should be nothing to pick between the two versions on content grounds. Ask them which one they would prefer to read. Hopefully, of course, they'll pick the one you want. But if you're dealing with a really horrendous stick-in-the-mud, ask them which one they think the end reader (customers, new employees, or whoever it may be) would prefer. This forces them to confront the fact that it's not being written to their own personal taste, but to help, or inform, or influence someone else. And if they're still being difficult, send them to me.

8. Being present

I've said that a lot of the techniques I'll talk about in this book are about making you – as the writer – more engaged in your writing, because I firmly believe that will make it more engaging for your reader. The problem with too much business writing is simply that it feels like it's been written on auto-pilot. It does the job; the usual words come out in the usual order and no one can really criticise it, but it doesn't really do any more than that.

A little while ago, I was doing some work with some actors. We were working with a group who wanted to improve the quality of their presentations (mostly, of course, written in the dreaded PowerPoint – more of which later). I was working with them on the structure of what they have to get across, and the language of it, and the actors were advising them on the performance of it. And the actors introduced me to the idea of *presence*, an idea I think applies just as much to writing as it does to performance.

They said that if you're on stage, there are lots of factors that might influence the quality of your performance – the audience, how well rehearsed you are, and all of that kind of stuff. But one of the big factors is much more about the actor's state of mind. They said that if you're having a bad day, or you're not interested in the play, or you've performed it a thousand times, you give a fairly workmanlike performance. Sure, you turn up, you remember your lines, you get your cues right, and you walk off stage through the right doors. But your brain, and your emotions, seem switched off. You're on the auto-pilot I talked about. You'll get the job done, but it won't be a Tony-award-winning show.

But on a good day, the actors said, you feel really *present*. You inhabit your character completely, and you're acutely aware of the other actors, the audience, and every single flutter of an eyelash you're making yourself. When you're present, you're entirely engaged in what you're doing.

> when you're present, you're entirely engaged in what you're doing

Writing is a performance, too

It might seem odd to think of writing in the same way as performance, because they seem like they might be opposites. In fact, I think they're really close. A good presentation is a projection of certain aspects of your personality in order to influence a room full of people. Often, the job of a bit of writing is pretty similar: engage someone, and get them to do something. The difference, of course, is that in person you don't just have the words to influence other people, you have lots of other stuff, too: body language, the tone of your voice, movement, interaction with the audience. When you're writing, you have none of that to help you out. Only the words can carry the personality as well as the content. Ironically, most people put *less* personality into their writing than they would into the words they use in a presentation – just when you need the words to do *more* work. To me, writing is about presentation. It's just a presentation you're not in the room to deliver.

So, just as you would in person, you need to be present in your writing; mind and emotions fully engaged. That's why lots of the techniques I'm talking about in this book will force you to think harder, by trying out different things – getting you off auto-pilot and into a different gear. Changing the order, using a metaphor, thinking of the rhythm; they all involve a change of mindset from our usual work writing mode. And if you're thinking harder, and your brain's more engaged, then you're going to be much more present in your writing.

Here endeth the lesson(s); time to get on with it. So, with all our expectations suitably managed, it's time to make a cup of tea, take your shoes off, and maybe even put your feet on the desk (don't worry, because this book's got *Business* in the title, when people see you, you'll get away with it – even at work), and have a read. Or dip in and out when you've got a minute, or when you're struggling. It should become the Gideon Bible of your workspace, lurking within arm's reach when you need a nudge in the right direction.

CHAPTER 2

Clunk, click, every trip

Or why there's always
some thinking to do before
you start

You know there are certain things you're supposed to do before you set off on a long trip in the car? Things that only a few of us every really get round to doing. Most of us these days remember to put our seatbelt on, but do we check the oil, check the water, pack an emergency triangle, and more importantly, an emergency sandwich in case we're marooned at the side of the road with only the sticky remains of a pack of Werther's Originals for sustenance?

Exactly: no, we don't. But we all know that we should. And one day, we all know that something bad will happen and we'll come a cropper because we haven't. We'll wish to high heaven that we'd packed that emergency sandwich.

Writing is the same. Yes you can launch straight in, lurching violently forward, hoping you'll reach the right point. And that's what most of us do; when we've got something to write, we just start writing. Sometimes we end up where we thought we were going, occasionally taking a wee detour on the way. Often, though, we find ourselves at the end of a bit of writing in a slightly different place to where we imagined, and not quite sure how we got there or if it's where we wanted to be.

So, like the car journey, to make the journey a little more straightforward, there are a few things we should do before we set off. And like the car journey, if you don't, most of the time you'll get away with it. But the more important the bit of writing – let's say the equivalent of a Formula One race, or a rally through uncharted territory – the more important the preparation.

And this preparation is mainly about structure: what you've got to say, what order you're going to say it in, and how you're going to lead your reader through. But even before you think of those things, you need to think about who your reader is, and what exactly they're interested in. So that's what our first few techniques are all about: planning, so that neither you nor your reader get hopelessly lost along the way.

preparation is mainly about structure

Who are you talking to?

brilliant tip

Have a real person in mind while you're writing, and it will make it more natural and vivid.

Do you know who you're writing to? Sometimes you will know exactly who's going to read what you've written, and that will help you tailor your content and your material. But sometimes you won't know. Sometimes you'll be writing to an audience of hundreds of people who you've never met; you might even be writing to people on the other side of the world.

The danger with not knowing your reader is that you stop thinking of them as real people, and start thinking of them as an amorphous mass. Because amorphous masses are difficult to characterise, we tend to bland out our writing, so instead of sounding like we're talking to lots of people, we sound like we're talking to no-one. And then your bit of writing is guaranteed to fail.

So, instead, you need to picture your reader. Now, if I'm really lucky, this book might sell 10,000 copies. But it doesn't really help me if I picture a sea of 10,000 people in front of me. In fact, it's quite scary. But if I picture one person – the sort of person who might come along to one of

> you need to picture your reader

my workshops, the sort of person I meet every day – then it becomes a lot easier to write naturally to them. I just imagine the conversation we might have.

You might never have met the sort of person you're writing to, of course. In which case, you have to do your best to imagine them. And I mean *really* imagine them.

brilliant action

Think about the answers to these questions for the person you're writing to:

- What's their name?
- Exactly how old are they?
- What newspaper do they read?
- What kind of education did they have?
- Where did they last go on holiday?
- What's their favourite TV programme?
- If they were at a train station, what sort of sandwich would they buy?

All of these things, even if they're made up, will help you treat them like a real person and not a cipher. This knowledge of your reader can have a marked effect on the way you write.

Let's take three British newspapers:

First, the *Sun*: tabloid, traditionally right-wing, famous for its topless 'Page Three Girls'.

Next, the *Guardian*: more highbrow, left-wing, the newspaper of choice for urban media types.

And lastly *Metro*: one of a number of papers all over the world now given out free to commuters on their way into work.

These are three very different papers with very different reader-ships, which you can recognise in the way that they're written. *Metro*, while good at making things concise (after all, it knows its readers might only have 25 minutes of reading time), is typically fairly bland. It's difficult to find a real opinion, or anything especially funny. It does the job, and it's not going to frighten the horses.

The *Sun* and *Guardian*, while written differently from each other, are both much more engaging in their own ways. More opinionated, with more of a sense of humour (designed to match that of their readers), and altogether more entertaining. And that's because they have a much clearer idea who their readers are. For a start, these are people who pay for the paper, so they must have quite a strong allegiance to the approach of their paper of choice. And so the journalists have a much more specific idea of the sort of people they're writing for – even if they're not that like the journalists themselves, and perhaps not even that likely to meet them – and so it's easier to get the right personality into their writing. That's why sussing out what newspaper *your* readers read in their own free time is a really good guide as to how to write to them.

What if you don't know who they are?

If you really don't have a clue what your reader is like, maybe you could follow the advice of Warren Buffett. As I write this book, Warren Buffett is the richest man in the world (despite giving most of his money away a couple of years ago to the Bill and Melinda Gates Foundation, thus doing his kids out of a massive inheritance. Brilliantly, he said he wanted his children to have enough money to do anything, but not so much that they could do nothing). Warren Buffett runs a company called Berkshire Hathaway in the USA, and is rightly famed for his investment nous. But he's also a brilliant writer. And I think those two facts are linked; he invests well because he's so clear in his thinking, and that also means he writes well. (I keep hoping this coincidence of skill with words and money will pay off in my own case, but here I am sitting in South London writing a book rather than sitting on a beach in the British Virgin Islands, so it looks like I might be waiting a little while longer.) Buffett is such a good writer that he was asked to write the introduction to the writing guide for the Securities and Exchange Commission. In it, he gives lots of (fantastic) advice on how to write for financial audiences. And this is who he says he's writing for:

> *One unoriginal but useful tip: Write with a specific person in mind. When writing Berkshire Hathaway's annual report, I pretend that I'm talking to my sisters. I have no trouble picturing them: Though highly intelligent, they are not experts in accounting or finance. They will understand plain English, but jargon may puzzle them. My goal is simply to give them the information I would wish them to supply me if our positions were reversed. To succeed, I don't need to be Shakespeare; I must, though, have a sincere desire to inform. No siblings to write to? Borrow mine: Just begin with 'Dear Doris and Bertie'.*

I find this fascinating. If you think about it, it doesn't seem quite to make sense. He's saying he writes for financial experts as if they're not experts at all, but as if they're his sisters. Now, logically, that doesn't sound like it should work as a technique. When people come along to the training sessions I run, one of the big things they worry about is sounding like they've dumbed down their material, or that they're patronising their reader. But if you read Warren Buffett, he sounds anything but patronising. Instead, he sounds like he's incredibly confident, and completely on top of his material. He sounds like he has no need to make things complicated, because he understands it so well. And he gives the credit for that to imagining his reader when he writes. Incidentally, one of the most successful companies of recent times is Google, and they've (unashamedly) copied a whole load of Buffett's techniques. Their annual report comes with a letter, written by one of the chief executives, to the shareholders:

> *Google is not a conventional company. We do not intend to become one... Sergey and I intend to write you a letter like this one every year in our annual report. We'll take turns writing the letter so you'll hear directly from each of us.*

(I wonder if they had Doris and Bertie in mind, too?)

Benefits, not features

When it comes to selling and marketing stuff, a particular aspect of thinking of your reader comes to the fore. It comes down to talking about what your reader is really interested in. If you've got a product or service to sell, and you know tons about it, there's a danger that when you talk or write about it, you'll just ramble on about what it does and how it does it. This is a particular danger for people in 'technical' trades, things like engineering, IT and the like. They blether on about the technical features of particular bits of kit, or particular methods, and unless you're talking to an audience who's very similar to you (by which I mean another techy supernerd), then they probably won't care two hoots. The secret, then, is to move from the features of what you're writing about to its benefits: what it will do for your reader.

> move from the features of what you're writing about to its benefits

There's a classic old marketer's trick to get people to think in the right way about this stuff: think of a banana. We could all probably name a fair few features of a banana: it's yellow; it's rich in potassium; it's curved. (There are people in my workshops who keep insisting too that it's a herb, but this book is way too short to get into that controversy here.)

Now, while all of those facts about the banana are true, they're not necessarily that interesting in themselves, especially if you were trying to sell someone a banana. Instead, you need to think of the benefits that go with each of those features. So, it's yellow: that means you can tell when it's ripe. Or that you can spot it in a crowded fruit bowl, if you're really in a hurry. It's rich in potassium: that means if you eat one, it'll keep you healthy (and specifically reduce your chances of hypertension, a quick Google search tells me). And it's curved: at a stretch you might say that means it fits in your hand; someone in my workshop even said, 'it's ergonomic'.

Now of course, not all of your readers will be interested in the same benefits. So you need to think what they're like, what they're worried about, what motivates them, and then hone your message to the things that are really going to float their boat. And this focus on benefits rather than features doesn't just help with products. It'll work when you're trying to convince people about a new initiative, or new ways of working. Anything where you've got to persuade people to do something they might not be otherwise inclined to do.

A sense of purpose

 **brilliant** tip

State why you're writing what you're writing very near the beginning.

I had a lecturer at university who used to make us start every essay we ever wrote with:

'In this essay, I will …'

and then we had to say what stuff we were going to write. Next, we had to write:

'I will show that…'

and then pretty much write what our conclusion was going to be, in the second line. Now, for most of my essay-writing education, both at school and at university, I'd been trained in padding things out, slowly working up to my conclusion, hinting at where I was heading, but not giving the game away. So what she was suggesting seemed crackers. If we told our reader what was in the essay, and what its point was, why would she read it? Nevertheless, she insisted, and after a bit of grumbling from us, it slowly dawned on us that we were writing essays that were tons better. And it's not surprising, because what she was doing, in essence, was to get us to write an 'abstract', a summary like that used by academics the world over at the beginning of an article or paper. And yes, that is the point of it: if you're flicking through an academic journal you get a really good sense of which bits are going to be interesting, original, or relevant to you, just by reading a few paragraphs.

And she recognised that in all likelihood, that first paragraph was the bit of our essay we were going to write first. So if we knew at the start of our writing that we had to know what we were going to say, and what the ultimate point of it was going to be, well then that did two handy things for our writing. First, we'd had to have had a pretty good think about our overall structure before we even took the lid off our fountain pens. But, most importantly, we had to have a very clear idea of the purpose of our writing, and to state it clearly. And that's something that's often missing from business writing.

It's amazing how often we don't state clearly *why* we're writing something. I think the reason is that by the time you actually sit down to write it, either you've done so much thinking in your head that it's pretty obvious to you what the purpose is (and because it's obvious to you, you forget to point it out to the reader); or, just as likely, is that, maybe under pressure of time, we

> it's amazing how often we don't state clearly why we're writing something

do our thinking as we're writing, so that we don't actually quite know what the purpose of what we're writing is until we've written it, and by then the deadline is looming, you've got ten other things to write, and frankly, you just want to move on.

The danger, of course, is that you leave your reader completely floundering. If they don't know why they're reading something, they probably won't be picking up on the things that are important to them – often things that will end up being important to you. Things like what you want them to start doing, or stop doing, or when they need to send your money in, or whatever it is.

This approach orients your reader, and looks like you've done some thinking on their behalf, so it can come across as quite generous-spirited. It might be something like:

This e-mail is about the three things we've changed about how we book holidays for people in the team, and what you need to do about it by the end of the week.

Having the purpose, the response you need, and the deadline right up front will focus the minds of people who do actually need to do something about your e-mail, and reassure those who don't have to react immediately about where your e-mail sits in the complicated food chain of their working priorities. So, everyone's a winner.

I should stress that your purpose doesn't necessarily need to come in absolutely the first line (as my lecturer insisted). Later in this book I'll be encouraging you to start in unexpected ways to send the signal that what you've got to say is worth reading. But if your purpose isn't in the first sentence, it needs to come pretty early on. And if you've written something and you spot the purpose lurking in the final sentence, that's when you know you've got some editing to do.

Automatic for the people

Lots of people get scared of a blank page (or more likely, a blank computer screen). Even as I type now, every time I stop to think for a second, the cursor is winking at me, expectantly. Come on then, it says, what are you going to say? Have you got anything interesting to write? What if it sounds stupid? (Not that that's stopped me before.)

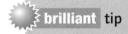

lots of people get scared of a blank page

Starting to write can be intimidating. Particularly because the beginning of whatever you write is always the most important bit, the moment where your reader decides to stick with you or not, or go and get their lunch. So it's not surprising that people get scared. If you're one of those people who can spend fifteen minutes staring at the blank space, here's something you can do.

brilliant action

Take a piece of paper, and give yourself a starting point that's a little bit related to what you've got to write about. Try to make it, though, a bit tangential or unusual; if you're writing about property prices, you might start, 'My home is important to me, because...'. Or if you've got an HR policy document maybe you could begin, 'The best day I ever had at work was...'. The more personal you can make the starting point, the better. And then once you've got that first phrase (and for heaven's sake, don't agonise about *that*, either), just start writing. But write automatically. Try not to think about it; write whatever comes into your head. You're not going to ever have to show this bit of writing to anyone, so don't edit yourself. Let whatever you've got to say come out. If your mind goes blank write 'the sky is blue', or 'I'm sitting in Tallinn airport' (that is literally what I'm doing now, as I write) and see where it takes you. It doesn't matter if you change subject completely, or if you think you're writing complete gibberish, just go with it.

Write like this for about five minutes (I suddenly feel like I'm writing a recipe book), or until you get sharp shooting pains in your wrist, whichever is the sooner. Then, take a deep breath and read back what you've written. Now, naturally, a lot of what you've done will be complete rubbish. But lurking in there might be an interesting idea, or an interesting phrase, or a way of looking at this subject that you hadn't really thought about before. Maybe, when you come to write your document for real, that could be your starting point. It will be probably more interesting than the starting point you would've chosen otherwise.

This technique is usually my slightly annoying answer to people who say they have problems starting to write; I mean, fundamentally the answer is 'just start writing'. But this approach does put you in a different frame of mind to the one we're usually in when we're writing. People who struggle to write usually struggle because they're putting too much pressure on themselves to get it right first time. And why would you get it right first time? It's rare that anyone's first draft is their best draft, that's why novelists, journalists and poets all have editors, to help them tweak their raw thoughts into perfection. So as soon as you accept that the first thing you write doesn't have to be the final version – or you write something that you know will never be the final version, like a bit of automatic writing – then you usually loosen up a wee bit. And because you've loosened up, you let a little bit more of your personality into your writing, and your approach usually becomes more interesting and more engaging.

> the first thing you write doesn't have to be the final version

And of course, if your automatic writing leads to complete and utter nonsense, then you've only wasted five minutes (or a wrist).

It started with a brief

brilliant tip

Make your brief brief, and interesting.

Many of us spend our working writing lives effectively writing briefs; defining things we want other people to do (or write). Or maybe, we spend our lives being briefed. In my job, I do both. So I wanted to say a word about how to approach these weird little things in particular. Briefing is a funny kind of getting started, because, essentially, it's getting someone else started. But you need to use all the same techniques you'd use if you were planning your own bit of writing: you need to think about the ultimate reader, and what they're interested in; and you need to be really clear about the purpose, thinking about the benefits and not the features. All of these things are going to be crucial if the person you're briefing is going to do the good job you want them to do.

There's more to a good brief, though. Often, we see a brief as a very functional document, setting practical stuff like constraints and budgets and word counts, or whatever your particular type of briefing demands. But a good brief has to do something of a sales job, too. After all, you want to motivate the person doing the work for you to do the best job possible. Ideally, you want them inspired about the challenge, thinking about it on the way home from work and jotting down ideas on random bits of paper when they wake up in the middle of the night. It's a competition, too. Because the person you're briefing might be working on umpteen other things at the same time. You want yours to be the one they think about first, or longer, or harder.

> a good brief has to do something of a sales job

The two secrets of brief-writing

First, it should be brief. That's why it's called what it is. Yes, you've got important information you need to get over, but you need to keep that to the bare minimum that person needs to do their job well. That's because you want them to know exactly the ground they've got to play with, but then just play. You don't want to hold them back or bore them rigid with everything you have ever thought of on the subject. If they need more information than the bare minimum, they will usually just ask.

And second, your brief needs to be interesting. Creative, even. I work with clients who worry that if their brief is too creative, then that's stepping on the toes of the people who'll be doing the work. Well, maybe. But I also know, as a writer, that the briefs I've responded to most creatively have been the most creative briefs. And that's because not only are they more interesting, and more motivating, they set an expectation, too. They say, we've made an effort here; we're interested in the project, and we really care about the result. As the person doing the legwork, it tells me that I have to make an effort, too. I have to be interested, and I have to care. So the better the brief, the more obliged I feel to deliver some good work in response. And that's exactly what the briefer wants.

So, with all of that mind, we should be thinking in the right way. Now there's just the small matter of what the hell you're going to say.

PART 2

Structure

CHAPTER 3

The order of events

Turning conventional
structure upside down

It started with a list

So, I've said that structure is thinking what you've got to say (and just as importantly, now you've been thinking hard from your reader's point of view, what you're *not* going to say). It's also about what order you're going to write things in, and how you're going to link from one bit to the next. We'll get onto thinking about what is the right order in a tick, but how do you get down what you've got to say at all? Well, I write a list.

I write a list of all the points I've got to make. Not in great detail; a sentence or even half a one might cover a paragraph, a page, or a whole chapter of the finished piece. But each sentence represents a main point I want to make. Sometimes I've had clients give very impressive names to this: 'developing the content plan', or even 'devising the copy platform'. But really it's just a list. The first list for this book was just a page long, listing the main sections and the main point in each one. As I've gone on, I've written a mini-list for each little chunk I've been writing.

Some people like doing this stage of a bit of writing on a piece of paper, just because the crossings-out and little arrows moving things round make them feel very in touch with the way that they're thinking. It's dead easy to do on a computer, though, particularly if you do want a play around with different orders, or be admirably ruthless and cut entire sections out with one determined stab of your typing finger. Armed with that list,

what if everything you learnt at school was wrong?

you need to settle on the right order for this multitude of points. Now you probably think you know the right order to write something in. But what if everything you learnt at school was wrong?

 **brilliant** tip

In a long document, put your conclusions first, before you go into the detail.

Stop writing up experiments

Remember how you were taught to write up science experiments at school? It's the first bit of formal writing training many of us had. Everything you wrote had to fit into one of a few (fairly dull-sounding) headings:

Aims

Apparatus

Methodology

Results

Conclusions

For many of us, every long document we write past the age of eleven is a rehash of that basic structure. Sure, the headings might change a little bit – *findings* instead of *results* maybe – but you're probably still writing pretty much the same thing today.

Now this approach has something going for it. It's very thorough; it shows exactly what you did and the order you did it in (unless you're me, setting the sleeve of my blazer on fire almost every time I looked at a Bunsen burner and desperately copying out someone else's results while a Petri dish quietly smouldered in front of me). And it feels very serious; this 'scientific method' was designed to make the experiment easy to repeat, and to make it feel objective.

There are two big problems, though, if you apply this structure to business writing today. The first is that while it may be easy to write like this, it's by far the slowest way to read something. Your reader has to wade through the whole lot of your report to find out what your conclusions are. And in most business contexts, they're usually the bit your reader is most interested in. They probably care more about *whether* you've decided to give them a 50 per cent discount than your precise reasons for doing so. The answer? Turn the order upside down.

Put your conclusions first. As I've said, you need to be a pessimist about your readers; they're only going to read the bare minimum they can get away with. The danger is that with this traditional, laborious structure, they'll stop reading before they get to the juicy bit – the bit you really need them to read. If you tell them your conclusions first, and they're happy with what they are, they can stop reading there and thank you for being so considerate of their time.

Of course, they might not be happy with your conclusions. In which case, you can keep writing about what you did and exactly how you got there, and they'll keep reading. Turning the structure upside down means only the readers with the real motivation to do so have to read the whole thing. The rest will read a line or two, and leave happy.

This approach also helps to deal with the second problem of this scientific way of writing, which is the *objective* style that comes along with this approach. Sometimes in business you'll want to sound calm and thoroughly dispassionate. More often you'll want to sound persuasive, or enthusiastic, or interesting. Tonally that's much less likely with the scientific method.

be a bit more
adventurous with
your structure

Subconsciously, these headings are going to steer you towards something a bit stiff. Be a bit more adventurous with your structure, and it'll let you loosen up your language, too. And in the next chapter I'll prove, not-quite-scientifically, why that's a Good Thing.

He dies in the first line

brilliant tip

Put your most important points at the beginning of what you're writing.

I've suggested putting your conclusions first because they're often the juiciest bit of what you're writing. And that's exactly what journalists do, too. They start with the juice. After all, they have the job of taking material they're not necessarily that interested in (and which is probably pretty similar to the stuff they wrote yesterday, or the week before) and turning it into something lively. In fact, when I'm feeling lacking in inspiration, I look at the papers. When you're writing that much every day, you know all the tricks that will help you turn something humdrum into something more interesting. And journalists use pretty much the same tricks, whether they're writing for a highbrow broadsheet or the commonest tabloid (that's why journalists quite often move from one to the other, or even write for both at the same time). They just change the balance of the elements that they use.

One of the tricks they use is 'the inverted pyramid'.

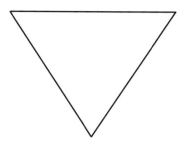

You can tell they're journalists, because actually the inverted pyramid is just a triangle, but this is what they're like – they can't resist hyping it up into something more dramatic. It works like this. Imagine there's a news story on the left-hand side. The inverted pyramid shows you how much fact to have at the different points in your story. So, at the beginning of the story you tend to get an awful lot of facts, and they tend to be the answers to the questions: Who? What? When? Where? Why? And how? So it might be:

A man was murdered yesterday, in Kennington, by his wife, after an argument flared over who should be the next mayor of London, while they were waiting for the bus.

(Kennington springs to mind because I live there, not because it's a notorious murder hotspot – though it is.) By the time you get to the end of the story, there's hardly any fact. Partly that's because you should have got all the big facts out of the way at the beginning of the story, so there aren't any left. But the end also tends to be full of the more emotive stuff; this is what a neighbour said, here's the mood on the streets now – that kind of thing.

Journalists use this structure for two reasons. First, and most importantly, they're pessimistic; they know that no-one reads the paper from cover to cover every day (unless you're in prison, or stuck on a desert island). We go through the paper, read little bits of stories, and decide which ones tickle our fancy enough to keep us reading. And we usually make that decision on the basis of headlines and first paragraphs. So the message from your editor is always to get the crucial facts of the story in at the beginning – the bits that will help people decide if the story is interesting or relevant to them (because they live in Kennington, or because they're particularly fascinated by the psychology of murder, for instance).

The second (slightly sneaky) reason is that this approach makes your story really easy to edit. Let's say you wrote your story at 12 noon, and by 6 pm that night a better story is breaking and they need to fit it into the newspaper. Well, if you really have followed the inverted pyramid structure, then your editor knows he or she should be able to cut the last paragraph of your story, because although it might be mildly diverting, it doesn't (or shouldn't) contain anything crucial. If you get a really ruthless editor, they'll keep chopping your story back, paragraph by paragraph, to see if it still makes sense. Woe betide you if you put some essential fact at the end of the fourth paragraph that's now been consigned to the daily tabloid dustbin. And every day when you see the paper, there's a column called something like 'news in brief' which is full of stories in little snippety paragraphs. Next time you have a look at them, think that probably many of them started off as much longer stories at the beginning of the news day.

What if it's not news?

While many of us in our business writing are not producing news, or even necessarily trying to write about facts in quite the same way, the inverted pyramid is a useful way of deciding where different elements should come in a longer bit of writing. You still need to say to yourself:

1 Which elements are absolutely crucial to what I'm writing?
2 Which elements are most relevant to my reader?

Those are the elements that should be coming first, or if not first, pretty high up in the story. If they're coming towards the end of what you're writing, there's a danger that your reader will just become that ruthless editor, deciding not to read the end of what you've written.

The stories that don't play along

Now the canny ones among you might be sitting there thinking, well, hold on, not all stories in the paper follow that structure. And you'd be right. This is the structure that papers use for news stories; if you read a feature (let's say the story of someone's life), the big important facts might not appear until later on (if it were the story of our Kennington murder, maybe our hero would only die three-quarters of the way through the piece). So how do they work? Well, features are usually longer, designed to be a much less immediate 'hit'. But they do still have the same problem of getting you hooked in the first place, and keeping you reading, which typically they do by getting you interested in the characters of the protagonists, and emotionally engaged in what happens to them, or what they think. In some ways, this is a form of writing which demands far more of the kind of writing tricks this book covers to get readers to stick with it. If you don't follow the structure of the inverted pyramid, your writing has to be even better. You need to make sure that you're pulling out all the stops to keep your reader awake and not wandering off to make a cup of coffee.

> make sure that you're pulling out all the stops to keep your reader awake

Another trick to nick

I said just now that we make our news story reading decisions on the basis of first paragraphs and also headlines. So while we're at it, there's another cunning thing to learn from the way that newspapers treat headlines, too. They use different sorts of headlines, depending on the type of story they've got. As I write this, I've got today's paper on the table in front of me (it's the *Guardian* of course, because I'm an urban, liberal, young professional stereotype). And, luckily, it's following the pattern. Typically, the stories at the front of the paper have fairly straight headlines that simply describe the main point of the story in very few words. So today it says:

> *Reports of up to eight dead as Chinese police fire on protesters*

and a few pages in:

> *Girl, 3, critical after fall from store escalator*
>
> *Snow forecast as cold front returns across country*

These headlines can afford to be factual, but fairly flat, because the editors are banking on the fact that we'll find the subject matter of these stories interesting enough that we'll read them without too much persuasion. In fact, that's why these stories are at the front of the paper, because the editor believes these are the stories that will be most important to the readers of this paper. By the way, the last one probably only works if you're British, and therefore obsessed with the weather, and likely to find trains – and probably most of the country's daily routine – derailed by a couple of inches of snow on a work day.

Move a few pages on in the paper though, and something funny happens:

> *Cornwall to Cumbria with not a penny to pay (if you're over 60)*
>
> *A glimpse through the Westminster keyhole*
>
> *Terminal mints and cheesy muffins*

From these headlines it's much less clear what these stories are about. And that's deliberate. Because they know that these stories are less intrinsically interesting, they've put them towards the back of the paper, and they're having to pull a few stunts to get you to read them. So these headlines are deliberately cryptic, intriguing, designed to tempt you to read something you might otherwise dismiss as being fairly unimportant in the grand scheme of things when you've got drop scones to bake or *Doctor Who* to watch on the telly. Incidentally, this approach even extends to first lines:

> *She said he stole a Chihuahua by sticking it in his jacket and was twice arrested for drunk driving, but yesterday Kathleen Turner issued a public apology to her former co-star Nicolas Cage...*

All for one and one for all

It's also worth remembering that on most newspapers, the people writing the stories don't write their own headlines. Sometimes in our business writing, especially when it's hard work, people think of writing as a very solitary activity. When people come into my office, because the company's called The Writer, people expect to walk into a library, hushed and full of intense and pale-looking scribes, hunched over their keyboards and tapping away in silence. Actually, it's not like that at all. Usually it's fairly noisy, with people reading stuff out to see how it sounds, or handing something to their colleague to see if they think the middle bit is getting boring, or saying things like 'Can you think of a good headline for this, 'cause I'm a bit too close to it?' And I think that's really healthy; there's no reason why writing is the sort of thing you have to do in solitary confinement. It can be collaborative. You can do it as a team.

> there's no reason why writing is the sort of thing you have to do in solitary confinement

That structure has been formalised in newspapers where journalists write the basic articles, and sub-editors check their work and write headlines. In fact, you will hear journalists talking about the useful 'tension' you can get between the way the original journalist treated the story, and the slightly different slant the 'sub' puts on the headline. So, on a tough day, when inspiration isn't striking, and you feel like you've been beavering away on your own for too long, ask the person next to you. It might take them 30 seconds to come up with the idea you've been looking for for the last half hour.

CHAPTER 4

I've been waiting for a sign

How to lead your reader through what you've written

Once you've decided on the points you've got to make, and the order you're going to make them in, that's the hard part of your structure sorted. But next you have to decide how you're going to convey that structure. You're going to need sub-headings of some kind, to help your readers suss out which bits are where (especially if you've boldly changed the traditional order in which those bits are going to appear).

Now, you could use the headings from the scientific experiment we've talked about: *conclusions, results, methodology* and all of that malarkey, which is what most of us instinctively do. The problem with those is that they're pretty flat, and a little cold (again, because scientific method-speak is designed

> your job is to engage your reader

to make things feel objective). But your job as a writer will not usually be just to write up a true reflection of events that will sound right in a court of law. Instead, your job is to engage your reader, getting them interested in what you've got to say.

So here's step one; a little tweak that will make what you've written feel a touch more engaging.

 tip

Try turning your sub-headings into questions. So:

Conclusions becomes: *What did we decide?*

Aims becomes: *What were we trying to achieve?*

Next steps becomes: *What do we need to do now?*

This has two advantages. First, as we'll see later, because questions feel more conversational you'll probably write the answers – the content sitting in each section – in a more direct and natural way. You'll probably write a little more personally, too. That's because to make the questions work, you've had to introduce a sign of who's talking, and who to – a *you* or a *we* has appeared. That's why most of us read sub-headings in the form of questions as more friendly and approachable.

If you're feeling really brave, you might want to move on to a third type of heading. Both the experiment style and the questions describe the content you're about to read, but they don't tell you what the writer is going to say about it. But that is possible. You could use your sub-heading to summarise the following content, rather than just describe it.

use your sub-heading to summarise the following content

Let's imagine you're briefing the British Prime Minister Tony Blair before the Iraq war, and recommending a course of action. You could structure it using the experiment headings:

Background
Conclusion

Or the question headings:

What's the situation in Iraq?

What should we do about it?

But you could also use your headings to sum up each of these points:

Saddam Hussein keeps ignoring UN resolutions*

Saddam should be removed by force.

(*Pick your own favourite justification here, of course.)

Now, these sorts of headings usually end up being a little longer. But, used well, they can be really helpful for a lazy reader. That reader need only read the sub-headings to get the gist of your argument. Indeed, you could take out those sub-headings and put them into your Contents page and they might not even need to read your document; they'd get a picture of every big thing you had to say right there. It's like extreme structuring. But it works. The longer your document, the bolder your tactics have to be to make sure your reader really takes on board what you've got to say (even if they don't read every last cotton-picking word).

> the longer your document, the bolder your tactics have to be

How Contents lead to contentment

 **tip**

Use Contents in lengthy documents of any format.

Books, particularly non-fiction (like this one), and particularly reference books, have *Contents*. That we all know. A list of all the things that are coming up. Newspapers can sort of have *Contents* too; quite often they'll give you a little bit of a story which is continued further on in the paper, or they might just give you a description of what you'll find later on, like 'TV listings'. It's pretty obvious why. If you're looking for something in a reference book, you don't want to read the whole thing to find the one nugget of information that you're looking for. Similarly, newspaper editors know however well written their daily rag is, we all just skip to the bits we want or need to know. Even websites do something similar. Usually one side of the page has a list of all the things on the site. You don't have to follow the set order, but you can pretty much see the big overall picture of the site on page one.

Now, if most of us were writing a long report at work, we'd probably include a *Contents* page. After all, that's what we're used to seeing in things like that. But how many pages would you be writing before you felt you needed one? Five? Ten? Actually, I'd argue that even quite short documents need *Contents*. In fact, *Contents* pages are going to come in handy in any situation where you think your reader might not read your every word (which is nearly always; we're being pessimistic, remember). If you've got a two-page document in Word, with really clear sub-headings so that the reader can see what's in each section, you might get away with no *Contents*. But you won't get away with it in an e-mail.

Because we've all been there. You get a really long e-mail from someone, containing tons of information, maybe even a few things they want you to do, but it's two pages long, you're busy and you just don't have time to read it properly. Chances are, you're going to miss something crucial. If you'd had some *Contents* list right at the beginning, you'd have a much better idea of where you were.

Yes, even in an e-mail

This approach is *especially* important in an e-mail, because often you can only see the first little chunk of it in your e-mail window, so you've got no idea how long it's going to be. Is Sally from Accounts going to do another one of her notorious five-page ramblers? You might not know without scrolling down a long way. That's just where *Contents* will help. Some people are weirdly squeamish about using

> you need a few tricks to make sure you get your point across

what they see as such a 'formal' technique in what is seen as a more casual medium. But as soon as any document, in whatever format, gets long enough that your reader might not read it all, then you need a few tricks to make sure you get your point across.

The way you write your *Contents* doesn't need to be long, or formal – just an indication of what's coming up, and in what order. If you're feeling particularly clever, you might even bring right to the top the deadline for any action, so your reader's in no danger of missing the fact that you might want them to do something. So it might look like this:

---

brilliant example

Your e-mail might look like this:

Hello folks,

Sorry for the long e-mail but there's three things I need you to know about:

1. *The problems we're having with expenses*

2. *How we're going to change the process*

3. *What your team needs to do*

*On point 3, I need someone in your team to get back to me **by the end of the week**.* ▶

You can go on to use those sub-headings in the rest of the e-mail, and your reader is going to be cock-a-hoop that you've made their life so easy (OK, their delight might not be up there with the birth of their first child, but they'll probably be quietly appreciative).

Feeling listless

brilliant tip

If you start writing a list, bullet point it.

A little one, this. But quite often, when writing, we're forced into writing a list. It might be a list of your skills on your CV, the things someone will get in addition to their salary if they take on a particular job, or the features of a new computer you're trying to sell. The trouble is, most of the time, lists are pretty boring. You'll be able to tell that as soon as you read it out, because your voice will usually drop, maybe get quicker, or just turn into a complete mumble.

There are two answers to this problem. First, you could keep your list short. Focus in on the few things that are most crucial. And when I say 'the few', I mean it. Most of the time, three things in a list work absolutely fine. That's because our brain can easily remember three things, and we're very used to hearing the rhythm of that, because the 'rule of three' is so established in our culture. You'll hear it everywhere, from radio ads to political speeches (from Caesar's '*veni, vidi, vici*' to Tony Blair and his 'education, education, education').

> our brain can easily remember three things

Four things in a list work well, too. It's still few enough that our brain isn't straining to retain the information, but four things also play with the expectations of our readers or listeners. The rule of three is such a tried and tested formula that flouting it – just by adding one extra element to the list – is ever so slightly disconcerting for your reader, and also a little bit intriguing. Somewhere in our heads there's a voice saying, 'you're only supposed to do three things in a list. What the hell is he playing at?' It's a tiny moment of tension, and that could be enough to keep them listening.

Sometimes, though, you will just have more things you need to put in your list than three or four. But we know your reader is likely to switch off as soon as you get to number five. So the thing to do then is bullet point the list, rather than writing it in prose. A reader who already knows what's likely to be in the list – or isn't interested – can then just skim right past it, and inwardly thank you for saving them a few seconds of their working life. A reader who's genuinely interested, on the other hand, can get all the information they need in a form that's dead easy for them to get their heads around.

brilliant tip

There's also a way to really get credit for helping your reader through a list. Before you write your list, tell your reader how many things are coming up in it. For instance:

You should use us to clean your windows for three big reasons:

1.　...
2.　...
3.　...

Use this trick, and it makes you look really in control. On some crazy subconscious level, your reader thinks 'Wow, he said there were going to be three things, and then there were! This guy's good!'

CHAPTER 5

Keeping it together

How to stop your writing running away with you

A long bit of writing can be pretty intimidating. There's a lot to think about: all the content, the order of it, and the actual writing of it. It's not a surprise then that lots of us get so intimidated that we put it off for ages, and then as the dreaded deadline approaches, it comes gushing out of us in a sprawling splurge of prose.

> a long bit of writing can be pretty intimidating

One way out of this trap is to change the way you think about this writing. My contract for this book says I have to write a minimum of 45,000 words. Now, if I sat down every Saturday and Sunday morning (which is when I'm writing) worrying about how I got from word zero to word number 45,001 (just to show I didn't do the bare minimum), I suspect I wouldn't get a lot written. I suspect it would spook me, or I'd lose the will to live.

But I've not been thinking of it like that. Instead, each weekend has been about a shorter 2,500-word chunk, which seems to me a much less scary prospect. It's much easier for me to craft 2,500 words at a time into something half-decent (well, you decide) than it is to try to keep in mind an overall picture of something much longer in my head. That's why most good long writing is actually lots of bits of really good short writing, all seamlessly stitched together.

> most good long writing is actually lots of bits of really good short writing

There's a danger with this approach, though, which you've probably spotted (though hopefully not by reading this book). While splitting something long into more manageable bits is good for the author's sanity, it could have a negative effect on the ultimate piece of writing. It could get really bitty, the equivalent of a book of short stories, perhaps; each fine on their own but not necessarily adding up to anything. A whole that's no more than, or even as great as, the sum of its parts.

But if you still want to write in this chunky way, the answer might be a theme; something that holds the structure of what you're writing together, by giving each bit something in common with the others and so linking together the different elements. I'm lucky that the idea at the heart of this book is a set of practical tips on different aspects of the writing process, which naturally fall into some big areas like structure and style, and then some smaller sub-sections within each of those categories.

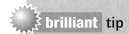 **tip**

Use a theme to link together shorter pieces of writing into a long one.

If what you're writing doesn't fall quite so easily, you might need to work a little harder. When we were writing a little book to introduce The Writer, we wanted to take just a few of the principles I'm talking about in this big one, and give a reader a little taste of our opinion on each. So at the beginning, we said the book was 'The 10 secret rules of business writing, with love from The Writer'. Each point we had to make, we found a way to make into a rule. This gave the book an overall feel, and made sure it didn't seem like we'd just made points at random.

They are:

1 *Start in the middle*

2 *Don't go on, please*

3 *Stop writing up experiments*

4 *There are only two types of writing*

5 *Bring your personality to work*

6 *Have an opinion*

7 *Thwack! (Or why we all need a surprise every now and then.)*

(There are only seven, because *The 10 secret rules of business writing* only contains seven, so that we could introduce the cheap trick of getting people to ring us up and find out the final three. In seven years, only one person has ever called our bluff. She was a *very* serious lady from the Inland Revenue who was just a bit baffled when I said we hadn't really thought what they were.)

We've just written another little book called *A Short History of Stickiness* for one of our clients. Again, they had a number of separate bits of content they needed to somehow yank and yoke together into a coherent whole. Their main point was about making their work stick, so each point was illustrated with the story of a sticky something – Sellotape, Blu-Tack, and the like – explaining how they work, and how they were invented. Not only did it help give the book an overall structure, but it also made it more engaging and more memorable.

Similarly, we often write proposals with a foodie theme. We write as if the different stages of a process are the starters, the main course and afters (or breakfast, dinner and tea). Once you've decided on a theme like that, you can take if further: get your reader to think of what you're writing as a menu for them to pick from (which it is). You can even invite them for a free taster, if you like.

> get your reader to think of what you're writing as a menu

The two techniques above both use metaphors to bring a theme to life, and we'll be coming back to metaphors later on. But the beauty of any theme really is not only can it bring potentially boring subjects to life, but it forces you to think hard about the structure of your end product before you start writing, and how you're going to link all of these disparate bits together.

CHAPTER 6

Death by PowerPoint: an antidote

Why one size doesn't fit all

Many of us write presentations as part of our jobs. Now, I don't want to talk too much about how to write them (not least, as there are whole books about the subject in this series). But there are a few big things that go wrong when people write on-screen presentations. Not for nothing do people talk about some aspect of their working lives as Death by PowerPoint.

> people talk about some aspect of their working lives as Death by PowerPoint

So, what goes wrong? Well …

1 **People don't think of an overall structure**. Instead, you get a download of every fact and stat they could think of, in an apparently random order. Your reader doesn't know what's coming, where you're heading or (most worryingly for them!) how long it's going to take.

2 **People put too many words on a slide**. That's because people use PowerPoint as a crutch, rather than a prop, so often on-screen you get the script for what they wanted to say to you in person. Now this would be reasonable (although pretty boring) if people just read that out. But they don't! What they do instead is they let you in the audience read the gazillion words they put on screen, while they recite a slightly different version of those words at the same time. Naturally it's nigh-on impossible to keep track of these two

things at the same time; it always makes me think of it like the bit at the beginning of Star Wars, that goes:

A long time ago, in a galaxy far, far away ...

Now, it's slightly tricky to read all of that stuff as it crawls across the screen. Imagine if there was someone (George Lucas, say, or an ewok) standing at the side of the screen at the same time trying to tell you a very slightly different version of the same story. It would drive you crackers – which, of course, is how most people feel at the end of most PowerPoint presentations.

3 **People write telegrams**. The other end of the spectrum is when people pare what they're writing right back to very few words. Usually, this works much better (especially if they're an entertaining speaker). But the danger is that on-screen, or when you're looking back on your notes after the session, it can all look a bit flat, or maybe a tad cold. That's because, in the righteous quest for brevity, people have a tendency also to squeeze out every last scintilla of emotion from what they've written. It can leave PowerPoint slides looking like a slightly severe telegram:

- Sales down stop
- People miserable stop.

keep the brevity, but just warm it up ever so slightly

The trick here is to keep the brevity, but just warm it up ever so slightly, usually with a touch of conversational language:

- Our sales our going down
- And that means people aren't happy.

But there's a more general PowerPoint problem, which is about what people use it for. It ends up being used for all sorts of different purposes:

> it ends up being used for all sorts of different purposes

1 The visual aid in the live presentation
2 The notes for people to read back after the session
3 Something to send round after the presentation for people who missed it.

Now, the thing is, if you write it to suit number 1, which is what PowerPoint is designed for, it's quite likely to be fairly hopeless for jobs 2 and 3. It'll be good for supporting the presenter and adding occasional emphasis and visual impact to the presentation, but it's not likely to tell a very good story out of context. If you write your presentation to suit jobs number 2 and 3, it's unlikely to do job number 1 very well, because there'll be too much information, which will fight with the presenter's spoken version of things. It might not even do job number 3 very well, as it's difficult to pick up the details of their argument through just a few key points without the narrative to hold it together.

By now, you've probably sussed out what my main point is going to be here. PowerPoint can't do all three of these jobs simultaneously and still be effective, because their purposes are very different. Try and combine them and you're always going to end up with a bit of a mess that doesn't do any of it that well.

The nasty answer is that jobs 2 and 3 are much better suited to a Word document, and a bit more prose. It'll probably take you longer to write, but it'll be much more useful for leading your reader through what you've got to say than just some bullet points. It's also why this book is a book and not a set of flashcards. And it's why my heart sinks when clients chirpily say to me, don't worry, I'll send you a document that will tell you the main bits of the brief, and I open up my e-mail – instead of a succinct, pithy, well-argued Word document, I discover that they've just bunged together 77 PowerPoint slides which only someone who's been working there for seventeen years can understand. It just doesn't cut the mustard.

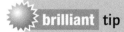 **brilliant** tip

Use PowerPoint for presenting, and Word for explaining.

PART 3

Style

CHAPTER 7

Doing what comes naturally

You already know the right style for your writing

So, with a bit of luck, now you know what you're saying, and what order you're saying it in. Next, the simple job of starting to write it.

As I've said, lots of us are pretty intimidated by starting to write, especially if we start writing at the beginning; usually that's where we're putting most pressure on ourselves to get it right first time. But in these word-processed times, there's no absolute need to start writing at the beginning; if you've planned your structure well, then you should be able to start anywhere and it will still work out OK in the end (the first

> start with a bit you'll enjoy, or an easy bit

page I wrote in this book, for example, was for the beginning of Chapter Three). So start with a bit you'll enjoy, or an easy bit.

And where are you going to write it? If your job forces you to write at your desk, then maybe you have no choice. But if you're lucky enough to have a laptop, then your writing can travel with you. Suss out what works best for you; I don't like writing anywhere really quiet because all I can hear are my own thoughts rattling round my head. So I put music on, or the radio. Or, get on a train. I've written a lot of this book on trains, because there's a bit of background noise, but not too many distractions like e-mails and TV programmes that want to be watched. Find the right length of writing time for you, too.

find the right length of writing time for you

I've enjoyed train rides of about an hour and a half because that's about the length of my attention span. I know that if I'm going to write for longer than that, I'll probably need a change of scene just to give myself a bit of different stimulus. So after an hour and a half, I move. Maybe to a café, or back home; just somewhere that stops me getting into a rut.

Now this all might seem very self-indulgent. But it's important that you feel comfortable as you write, because that will come through in your writing. The best writing usually sounds natural, and relaxed, so that's how you should be feeling.

Natural. It's a word that keeps, and will keep, cropping up in this book, because for me, it's the key to style. We've already talked about some of the big things to think about when it comes to style: writing more like you speak; being more than just plain. What a lot of it comes down to is naturalness. Most of us are at our best when we're at our most natural: clear, human, engaging. And those are exactly the qualities we want to get into our writing. Plus it means that your own personality will shine through. After all, while we might work with people who are similar to us, hopefully they're not exactly the same. The best writing has that individual stamp that reassures you as the reader that there's a real person behind it.

most of us are at our best when we're at our most natural

After this talk of naturalness, it feels odd then to say that there are techniques that we can all use. Surely, if we all started using them, we'd all sound the same? Well, I doubt it. We all use them in different ways, and in different proportions. But the hints and tips in this chapter are really about finding the naturalness that most of us have had drilled out of us by education and corporate life. Instinctively we know what's natural, but it gets masked by institution-speak and what's thought of as a *professional* approach.

Well, the revolution starts here: it's time to break out. A little bit, anyway.

Don't take that tone with me

 **tip**

Pick words that reflect the spirit or personality of your organisation.

Hello.

What would you think if I met you and I said *hello*? Not much probably; it would probably be exactly what you'd be expecting to hear. No surprises. How about if I said…

Hi!?

You'd probably think very slightly different things about me than if I'd just said *hello*. It's a trick I pull in workshops. And most of the time when I'm at work, I haven't put a tie on, I'm wearing a shirt, but I've not tucked it in. I might even be wearing my trainers (or sometimes my black trainers that look like proper work shoes, but aren't really). And, together with my saying *Hi*, on seeing me, you might make some conclusions about the sort of person that I am. Or, perhaps, the sort of person that I'd like to come across as. You might even have started to ask yourself: Is he going to be interesting? Do I like him? Does he know what he's talking about? But those aren't my only two choices. I could've said…

Yo!

or

Yo! Respect.

And probably I would've lost your attention at that moment, because if you saw me, you'd know that even though I live in South London I can't quite pull off something quite so gangsta. But if you think about it, all of these ways of starting a conversation mean exactly the same thing. The content is identical, but which one of them you choose to use says something about your personality, and starts to shape the way your reader takes on board what you've got to say.

> which one of them you choose to use says something about your personality

Of course, that impression you create might be a reflection of your own personality, but it might also be a reflection of the personality of the company or the organisation that you work for. After all, most of us, when we get into the office, don't behave – and therefore, write – exactly as we would if we were our own boss. We take on some aspect of the culture and values of the place we're working – hopefully not to the exclusion of our own personalities. Probably we end up with something of a compromise between how we'd say something and how we think our organisation should say it.

These differences come out in quite basic ways. If I get a letter from BT, Britain's biggest telephone company, it usually starts:

Dear Mr Taylor,

but if I get a letter from Richard Branson's Virgin, who compete with BT to sell phone lines, broadband and TV packages, it starts:

Hi Neil.

Right there in the those first two or three words, those brands have told you something about their attitude, their approach, and probably the sort of customers they're interested in (lots of people tell me they hate the palliness of Virgin, but their customers are usually pretty comfortable with it).

At The Writer, we call this 'tone of voice' – defining the style of language that fits with the culture of your organisation or your brand. So, when you're writing, it's worth thinking if that spirit is reflected in the words that you're using. The values or mission statements are often a good starting point. If one of your values is *straightforward*, you should be looking to try to cut out the jargon, caveats and legal terms and conditions. If your organisation says it's *passionate* (and lots of them do – companies that do all kinds of dull things I'd find it difficult to get passionate about), then think to yourself, do I sound passionate? Faced with a brief like that, I'd be looking to get my enthusiasm across though opinions and stories rather than just *saying* I'm passionate.

> values or mission statements are often a good starting point

How does it work in practice? Well, one of our clients at the moment says they are *bold*. But not bold in a shouty, brash, in-your-face kind of a way. They mean they're bold in that they've got a quiet confidence, and at the same time aren't afraid to do unusual things. So we're encouraging them to really pare back what they've got to say to very few words, and to use words which are surprising, emotional, even a little bit poetic at times. That feels like a quietly bold way of writing to us. Or, another client of ours says they're driven by their strong set of beliefs. So we've encouraged them to use lots of sentences to explain how what they do is related to what they believe:

We do X… because we think Y…

That way, their language will reflect the spirit of their organisation.

Your organisation may not have gone to the lengths of defining its tone of voice – or even its brand – though more and more are. But if you stop to think about it, you probably have a fairly instinctive sense of how your organisation would like to come across. Indeed, some of the brands with the most distinctive tones of voice don't ever have to define what they should sound like, because it's just a natural, intuitive reflection of a strong internal culture, or even the recognisable personalities of the founders (I think this is the case with Richard Branson and Virgin, or the three lads who founded Innocent Drinks in the UK).

So if you think your writing is competent, but all of your competitors would write exactly the same thing, you need to think about what's really distinctive about the spirit of where you work, and how you can get that to come across in the way that you write.

think about what's really distinctive about the spirit of where you work

CHAPTER 8

Word perfect

Why every word matters

The Battle of Jargon

When I go in to talk to people about their business writing, and ask what's wrong with the way they do it in their organisation, the first answer is usually 'it's full of jargon'. And as people say it they tend to sigh, the stress starts to tell in their voice and their body gets all tense. It's clear that jargon is something that winds a lot of us up.

> jargon is something that winds a lot of us up

Yet clearly a lot of us use it. Why, if we profess to abhor it? Well, first, I think we need to define what jargon is.

brilliant definition

To me, jargon falls into two camps:

1 **Specific technical vocabulary**
   Nearly every sector, and sometimes every company within that
   sector, has terms which have either been invented or redefined to
   mean something specific to the people in that particular line of
   work. Every sector has them. In my past life in marketing,
   people talk about *propositions*, *brand equity*, and *customer
   journeys*. I'm working with social workers from a county council at
   the moment and they talk about *care packages*, being
   statemented, and *client's needs* – and they mean something quite
   specific; they don't mean the things that we would probably
   guess at.

2 **Business buzzwords**
   This is a second category which is much less specific; you tend
   to find these words across different sectors, and they've become
   a marker of 'business language'. I'm talking about *end of play*,
   leverage, and the like. These are usually images – metaphors or
   similes – originally designed to make the language more vivid.

I think we need to treat these two jargon groups quite differently.

The first group, at its best, is useful shorthand. It helps you
communicate something quickly that might otherwise take you
a relatively long time to explain every time. In an ideal world,
join a new company or start working in a new sector, and you
should be able to pick up a glossary of those words, learn it,
and once you've got it you should be
able to cut it among your new-found
colleagues. The trouble is it's rarely
as simple as that. First, after a while,
you start to discover that sometimes
people mean different things when
they're using the same words.

> sometimes people
> mean different things
> when they're using the
> same words

When I worked with the UK educational quango, the Learning and Skills Council, there was very nearly a round of fisticuffs when I asked exactly what a *framework* was. Every team that was represented in the workshop all had their own definition, and thought the other lot's definitions were insane. Of course, they were never going to agree, because it's a metaphor, not a specific bit of terminology. They all knew what a framework was literally – they'd all climbed up them at school – it was just hard to be so definitive when it was used figuratively.

My own industry is just as afflicted, which is a shame, considering that it's supposed to be made up of people who are good at communicating. It is riddled with brand pyramids, essences, positionings and propositions. The problem is that no two clients I've worked with have ever defined a *brand proposition* in quite the same way. Given that situation, you'd think the obvious thing for people working in brand and design agencies would be to ask the people using the words what the heck they mean. But that happens all too rarely, because most of the time people in those agencies are too scared to ask them.

Why? Because they're worried that just asking the question makes them look thick. They think the client will say 'This person works in marketing, and they don't even know what a *brand horseshoe* is? Jeez, what a schmuck.' Luckily, being a writer gives you licence to ask all sorts of supposedly dumb questions in the name of research, because you can often claim it's not your specialist area. And when you do, a curious thing can happen. It turns out that often the people writing these words don't know what they mean either.

So, right there are two of the big problems of jargon. People use it to look like they know what they're talking about, even when they don't. But throw in a few acronyms or technical multi-syllables and you can con people into thinking you're an expert. Get the jargon right, people think, and I'll waltz my way in among the middle management. That's why the people who are *really* good don't need to use it – they're not worried about proving anything. They know they're experts. And they know their ideas and opinions are strong enough that they don't need special words to prove it.

The other problem is, because it's so common, people can become completely inured to it. Write a paragraph peppered with jargon and acronyms, and your reader will tend to tune out, even if they understand it all. Sometimes though, they'll just ignore it completely. A little while back, I did some work with a big division of a UK oil company. The chief executive of this division decided that this year was the year of *operational excellence*. So when you walked into the office, behind the reception was a huge sign that said *operational excellence*. In the canteen, on the walls, it said *operational excellence*. In your appraisal, you were measured on how *operationally excellent* you were personally. Your working day looked pretty much like this:

> write a paragraph peppered with jargon and acronyms, and your reader will tend to tune out

operational excellence

operational excellence

operational excellence

operationally excellent.

So they let this campaign roll, and after six months they looked at the numbers of whatever it was they'd been measuring, to make sure they were having exactly the impact they wanted. And when they did, what difference had it made? None. Nothing. Nada. Zilch. Despite the time and money they'd poured into it, no one had done anything differently, it seemed.

Except for one team.

There was one team where everything they wanted to improve had improved. One single, solitary place that had achieved what they'd hoped the whole business would achieve. So they went to the person running that team, and naturally enough, asked him what he'd done. How had he managed to succeed where everyone else had failed? His answer was simple. Instead of banging on about *operational excellence*, he explained that he'd run a weekly meeting with the title *doing everyday things better*. And true to the spirit of the programme, he'd just translated *operational excellence* into everyday language. He'd made everyday communication better.

And that's the danger with this sort of language. In theory, everyone at this company knew what *operational excellence* meant, but somehow the type of language made it too easy to ignore. It had become abstract, corporate white noise which we tune out so that we can get on with our jobs. The way round it is to ask yourself, 'What do I really mean?' And when you've done that, and come up with a better way of saying it, ask yourself again. See if you can

> see if you can make it even more straightforward

make it even more straightforward. I find it can take me a few goes to push a bit of classic corporate blah into something that really is clear.

And if you really have to use jargon, at the very least you could own up to the fact. I was recently doing some work with the UK financial services firm Standard Life. I was getting them to rewrite a letter that said something like:

Thank you for your request for the surrender value of your policy

I don't know if you'd understand that, even if you'd asked for one. When I asked people what it meant, people usually suggested something like *Thanks for asking how much your policy would be worth if you cashed it in* (which is more like what most of us would actually say). Quite often we then had an argument about whether we could say *cash in*, given that it's unlikely Standard Life would be sending anyone a wad of used fifty-pound notes in the post. I stood my ground, and won my argument that just because we say *cash in* doesn't mean we're literally expecting cash. But then someone came up with a much more technical argument. He said, 'We need to say *surrender*, because there are different ways of cashing in a policy. Surrender is a very specific one, and we need to be clear from a legal point of view which one we mean.' Damn, I thought to myself. But someone very canny in the workshop then wrote:

> *Thanks for asking how much your policy would be worth if you cashed it in (technically, this is known as 'surrendering' it).*

I thought that was brilliant. A really good way of using the jargon your company or industry forces you into, but thinking first of all about the reader. I think you'd really warm to that writer (and their company) if you got that letter, because they look like they're falling over themselves to be helpful.

Back to the buzzwords

The second type of jargon is more pernicious, I think. It's less essential, certainly. It doesn't usually convey any kind of specialist knowledge. Instead, it's designed just to make the writer (and more often, speaker) look like they're very up to date with the latest business thinking. The trouble with this kind of language, though, is that it's not often communicating anything particularly sophisticated or original; again it's more about signalling your membership of the MBA club.

Now, don't get me wrong; I'm not saying that I object to this kind of language just because it's not as simple as it could be. After all, I'm a writer. It's my job to make things sound different, interesting and more lively. And in fact, the first time someone came out with these phrases, they must have sounded startlingly fresh. The first person to say not *Let's talk about this idea, and see who's interested,* but:

Let's run it up the flagpole and see who salutes

must have sounded pretty cool and creative. So much so that millions of people decided to nick the phrase and use it as their own.

But there's a well-studied phenomenon in language where anything which is used too much loses its impact. Here are two examples. Those of you who speak French will know that you use *ne... pas* to make something negative:

> anything which is used too much loses its impact

Je vais: I go

Je ne vais pas: I don't go

Now originally only the *ne* bit was negative. The *pas* originally meant *a step*, and was added to negative forms of verbs like *go*, *walk*, and *run* to give them a bit of emphasis: *I did not walk a step.* But it became so common that French speakers started using *pas* with other verbs where *not ... a step* made much less sense, verbs like *to eat* or *to sleep*. But *je ne mange pas* doesn't mean *I don't eat a step* (which would be strange). The *pas* just became an automatic part of the negative, without adding any emphasis.

What will offend us next?

The same thing's happening with swear words in British English. Swear words in most cultures tend to relate to what's most taboo at the time. We Brits spent a good few centuries a good deal more religious than we are now, so church-related or blasphemous swear words were pretty shocking to our God-fearing sensibilities. But with the Victorians, sex became much more of a worry. Words that had been perfectly everyday for hundreds of years suddenly became frowned upon, and they're the words we're pretty much still using today when we really want to get a reaction. Arguably though, since the Sixties, even those words have lost their bite. So, in mildly geeky linguistics circles, the betting's on as to where the next set of swear words will come from in English. My money's on racist terms starting to be used out of context, because they're the most unacceptable things we can express in polite society at the moment.

In a working context then, these buzzwords are the exact equivalent. Their frequency means they too have lost their power. Instead of startling new thoughts, they've become corporate clichés. So much so that people all over the world sit on conference calls playing 'boardroom bingo' (that's the polite version of the name, anyway), seeing how many laughable phrases their colleagues can rack up in the course of one meeting.

> people all over the world sit on conference calls playing 'boardroom bingo'

As soon as they reach that point, because they're so expected, look at them alongside their more everyday alternatives, and they're neither clearer, nor have more impact. That's why we shouldn't use them. So, my advice is: stick to the simple equivalents, or even better, come up with a cool new phrase yourself. And the minute anyone else copies you, stop saying it.

> come up with a cool new phrase yourself

 **brilliant** action

Purge yourself of your inner jargon

Make a list of two things:

1 all the jargon that's associated with your job
2 the buzzwords and phrases you or your organisation are prone to using.

When you've filled up a side or two of A4, have a look at it all together. Ask yourself a few questions:

1 Does every one of your readers always understand what you mean when you use it?
2 Do you always understand what you mean when you use it?
3 If you were explaining it to someone who'd never heard it before, what would you really say?
4 If you used that version, would your writing feel different? How?

Do you speak Latin or German?

brilliant tip

> Avoid Latinate words that can sound pompous or pretentious.

If you're a native speaker, you already speak both. Well, kind of. Because of the way the English language evolved, we have at least a couple of alternative words to express most ideas. And which one you choose could make a big difference to the impression that you create.

Take two words like *freedom* and *liberty*. Can you explain the difference to me? Probably not; and even if you succeed in giving it a shot, your answer is going to be pretty damn subtle. But they do have a different feel, and that's to do with their different histories.

English is basically a Germanic language. Lots of Germanic peoples like Angles, Saxons and Jutes hopped across the North Sea to England, speaking versions of the language that also eventually gave rise to German, Dutch and all the Scandinavian languages. And most of the most frequent words we use are still pretty similar to those words we inherited 1,500 years ago from these German invaders.

And then there was a pesky invasion: 1066 and all that. All these Normans turned up, speaking an early version of French, and suddenly became Lords of the Manor all over the country, as well as clergymen, lawyers, officials, and the like. Because of all these French speakers in influential positions, the Germanic base of English was added to with loads of words we 'borrowed' from French, especially those related to the 'sophisticated' professions above. All of these French words ultimately started off in Latin, and, later, educated types nicked even more stuff directly from Latin itself.

All of this borrowing has left English with a hodge-podge of a vocabulary, with often two words for nigh on the same thing, with two different origins. For example, one notable quirk is that, unlike most European languages, we use different words for animals and the meat that comes from them. We feed *cows* but eat *beef*; we look after *sheep* but eat *mutton*; watch the *pigs* playing in mud but eat *pork*. That's because we kept the Germanic word for the animals, but started using the French ones for the meat (because they're better at cooking than we are, or were).

How does this linguistic history lesson affect business writing? Well, the language of business writing evolved from that of legal language, which was traditionally dominated by French and Latin (when the British Queen agrees to a law, for instance, she still makes that happen by writing *la reine le veult,* an old Norman French way of saying 'the Queen wills it'). And we're still suffering from this linguistic hangover. Somehow, when people swap into business mode, they reject the Germanic words they use in everyday speech, like *start* or *do,* and instead pick one of the apparently more 'professional' sounding French- or Latin-based ones, like *commence* or *action* (as in 'I'll action that later').

> the language of business writing evolved from that of legal language

Now, I like French (I did a fair bit at university), so I don't have any kind of ulterior motive for saying what I'm about to say. But given the choice of these two options, most of the time I'd go for the Germanic one. One of the big themes of this book has been how you get your writing to feel natural, because that makes you sound like a real person, and that makes the businesspeople you're dealing with warm to you. And because the Germanic options here are the words we usually pick in everyday conversation, they're the ones that are going to sound the most natural. After all, you've never said to the kids:

Make sure you finish your tea before you commence watching the telly.

Take Bill Clinton. One of the reasons he got himself into such hot water over his fling with Monica Lewinsky was the language that he chose to talk about it in. In his evidence, he famously said:

...I did not have sexual relations with that woman...

Now, quite apart from the disdain of **that** *woman,* which certainly didn't endear him to many of his listeners, think about the phrase *sexual relations.* It's very far away from everyday language. It sounds at best euphemistic, and at worst deliberately cold and aloof, and that's because it's using quite formal, Latinate words, words with an inherent sense of distance. This distance may have been handy in a court of law, but to the bigger jury of electors it sounded inhuman, and given the warmth and charisma of Clinton's public pronouncements up until that point, almost deliberately weasly. So in this linguistic battle, I'm on the side of the Germans.

 **action**

Become a Latin translator

Think of the everyday (Germanic) equivalent of each one of these Latinate words:

terminate
significant
consult
request
demonstrate
prohibit
alter
amend
endeavour
attempt
volition
inconvenience
receive
donate
circa
approximately
notify
inform
resolve
administer

Compare the originals with the new versions. How do they feel different?

Binning the legalese

 **brilliant** tip

Avoid words that sound too legal or formal.

And there's another set of doublets you have to choose from, too. Because business writing evolved from legal language, we again have a choice; between a 'normal' word and a quasi-legal one. Have a look at this list:

The legal one	*The normal one*
Therefore	So
Thus	So
However	But
In order to	To

The words on the left aren't confusing or anything like that, but they're hardly ever used in conversation, so they'll make you sound like you're trying to sound stuffy. Now I know many of you will be taught that you should never write the word 'but'. That's rubbish, as we'll discuss in a wee while. And the supposed prohibition of 'but' is just an extreme version of the way all of the words on the right are treated – like written poor relations, even though they're the fundamental building blocks on which most natural speech is built. Of course, there

read it out loud, and see how it sounds

will be occasional situations when you really would use one of the fusty ones on the left when you're speaking. But rarely (see – 'Rarely, however' would've sounded terribly pompous there).

So the check, as always, is to read it out loud, and see how it sounds. If it sounds slightly forced, or worse, if you're putting on a voice (probably the voice of a solicitor from Surrey) to help you get away with it, then it's not the right word.

 **action**

Become a paralegal

Think of the everyday equivalent of each one of these legalistic words, and again, think how they feel different:

prior to
in advance of
aforementioned
regarding
with regard to
notwithstanding
hereby
at the present time
on behalf of
such as
in the event that
in accordance with
monies
arrears

Get personal

 **tip**

Use personal pronouns like *I*, *we* and *you* wherever you can.

Your country needs YOU!

Ask not what your country can do for you, ask what you can do for your country.

I have a dream today.

We shall fight on the beaches, we shall fight on the landing grounds, we shall fight in the fields and in the streets, we shall fight in the hills; we shall never surrender.

A few famous lines from some of the most powerful speeches and posters in history, lines that still resonate today even though their subject matter can feel like it's a long, long way off. And while these lines were all written about different things, and by different people, they all have something in common. They all use personal pronouns (words like *I, we, you*) to talk directly to the reader, or to put the writer in the centre of the action.

Now this is something that most organisations have got a lot to learn about. Lots of the ones I work with talk about themselves (and their customers) in the third person, as if they weren't speaking themselves, and they weren't speaking directly to their readers or listeners, either. Let me give you an example. The other day, I was at a train station, and heard an announcement that went roughly like this:

South West Trains would like to apologise for the delay to the 19.15 service. Customers should take the next train and change at Clapham Junction for London Waterloo.

Now, if you were talking, this is not how you'd put a message like this across. Instead, you'd probably say something like 'We're sorry that the 19.15 service is late. If you're heading for London Waterloo, you should take the next train and change at Clapham Junction.' Apart from some of the sneaky changes I've made to make some of the vocabulary less formal (like swapping *sorry* for *apologise*), the biggest change is the way I've described the different people involved. In both cases, the people talking are the train company. In the first version, they use their own name, South West Trains; in my version, I use what we would all naturally use in conversation: *we*. Likewise, the people they're speaking to are *customers* in the first version, *you* in the second. To my ears, it sounds more natural, and more genuine.

Yet loads of businesses talk about themselves in the third person. We all know this sounds funny, because when people in the public eye do it, we have a chuckle at their starry pomposity. If Madonna were to say 'Madonna doesn't do interviews,' it would sound as if she believed herself to be such a phenomenon that she has somehow ceased to be a real person, and is instead an icon, an idea, a brand. It sounds absurd.

> loads of businesses talk about themselves in the third person

So nearly everywhere I work, I advise people to refer to the organisation they're working for as *we*, or if they really are referring to themselves, then *I* is the thing to go for (in fact, used right, it can be really powerful – it can imply real responsibility and authority). But in my workshops, people come up with all kinds of spurious reasons as to why they can't do it. And I think they're all nonsense. They say things like…

1 **The reader won't know who the *we* is**. Well, nine times out of ten people are writing documents in templates with the organisation's logo all over the letter, report, website, or whatever it is that's being written. Most of us in that situation would assume the *we* refers to that organisation.

2 **They don't want to be identified as being part of the *we*.** I've worked with people in quasi-governmental organisations whose job it is to produce policy. One person explicitly said to me, 'I can't write *we*, as in *we consider that this is the best course of action*, because I don't; I disagree with the policy,

but it's my job to write it.' Well, I understand this chap's pain. But his problem here is not really a linguistic one, it's a moral one. Just getting rid of the *we* doesn't absolve him of responsibility. His reader won't understand the subtlety of his position from his writing (although, in my experience, they may well pick up on a vague sense of unease which will make his writing seem less confident, and less effective). If you're writing on behalf of the organisation, in your reader's eyes, you *are* the organisation, unless you choose to write *I* (which would've been even less likely in this situation). In fact, the organisation is nothing but the people in it. So if you are so desperate to distance yourself from the organisation and its decisions, you should probably just get another job.

3 **It's more objective**. Then it's back to this old chestnut. Loads of us still have in our head that we're supposed to be writing objective documents, which don't betray the point of view or the emotions of the author. But most of the time we aren't writing scientific treatises. Most organisations have what you might see positively as a point of view, or an attitude, or what you might see negatively as a bias. But however you see it, it's just true. The most straightforward thing you can do as the writer is own up to that bias, and allow your reader to judge. Eliminating that personality also eliminates the possibility that you might win them over with your charm, wit, or strength of character; all difficult things to get across if you're trying to be objective. In fact, if you're writing on behalf an organisation with a strong brand, then you really have to go for it. Brands only work if they really stand for something different to their competitors. An objective brand is a bland brand, or not a brand at all.

4 **It's not true**. Occasionally, people argue that they're genuinely not part of the *we* who's talking. They say, 'I can't write *we'll get back to you* because it's someone in a different team, not mine. And I've no idea if they're really going to do it or

not.' This is really just another version of number 2. Even if you know you're different entities, your reader probably doesn't. The reader sees your organisation as a generic *you*. That's why, when we ring call centres, and companies tell us 'I can't help you with that, you'll have to ring another department,' it drives us up the wall, because we think their internal structure is their problem, not ours. Do you think Winston Churchill was going to fight anyone on the beaches? Of course not. By all accounts, he'd often had a glass or two, even if he'd been young and fit enough to take part. If you think of it in business terms, it was a well and truly different team who were going to do the fighting. But his *we* in that speech was all the more powerful because he was identifying himself as part of the armed forces, or maybe speaking on behalf of the British people, if you choose to read it like that.

In a little while, I'll also talk about rewriting passive sentences into active ones, where that's what we'd naturally say (don't worry if you don't know what I'm talking about yet; it'll make sense soon). This also forces a bit of more personal writing out of you, because instead of saying things like 'This will be implemented in June,' you actually have to commit as to who's going to do it. Is it we? Is it I? Is it – shock, horror – you?! There's a laudable explicitness there that will save you getting into hot water later on.

Verbs not nouns

brilliant tip

Don't write nouns where you'd use a verb if you were speaking.

The other day, I was walking down Shaftesbury Avenue in London's West End. Just as I was getting close to the road junction at Cambridge Circus, I saw a sign – a sign that stopped me in my tracks. It said:

Pedestrian

Casualty

Reduction

Signal Timings

Experiment

I was perplexed. What did it mean? Was it just six words that some signwriter knew, and was determined to show off to us about it? Which one went with which? Was it some kind of urban poetry? It was dented, as if it had been hit by a car, or maybe by an unlucky flying pedestrian who'd got a bit distracted trying to work out what the hell it was going on about.

I think what they meant was 'We've changed the sequence on the lights.' That is, if you're used to driving down this road, and you know that ten seconds after the cars in the other direction have stopped, it's your turn to go, watch out. The lights aren't going to go how you expect them to.

But somehow, this sign doesn't say that at all clearly. It has come out in Department-of-Transport-speak, and as a result spectacularly fails to do the job it's meant to do. And there are a number of things that make it hard work. It's too long; the fact that they're trying to bring down the number of accidents is laudable, but it's not something I need to be being told in the split second before I arrive at the junction. It certainly shouldn't be the first thing that I see.

It's got jargon in it. The word *signal* here means traffic lights. *Traffic lights* is what everyone in the entire UK calls those things. But somehow these civil servant jokers – despite the fact that it's their job to communicate things about transport – have completely forgotten that that's what a normal person would say. *Signal* could be anything: semaphore? A beacon on top of a hill? Two fingers? It's the *lights* you mean, you fools, *lights*!

You wait forever for a bus ...

But I think the biggest problem with this sign is a more 'linguistic' one, if you like. Part of what makes this so difficult to decode is the fact that this is six nouns in a row. Remember nouns from school? Words which represent objects or ideas. They're useful, of course (like the words *words*, *objects* and *ideas* in the last sentence). But they're conspicuously much less helpful when you get six of them at once. Like buses, you'd be perfectly happy with just one, at the right time. It's the fact that this is a string entirely made up of nouns that has allowed the writer to add in all those capitals, which don't help either. It ends up looking like Middle English.

But the problem really is that this string of nouns is very far away from how we would naturally speak. If you're explaining this to someone in person, you'd use a lot more verbs ('doing words' they were called at school). You might even say something like

*We've **tried changing** the timings on the lights to **stop** people **getting hit** by cars*

Yes, it's more words, but it's also easier to understand more quickly because it's closer to what we're used to hearing. Yet this over-reliance on nouns is a classic feature of business writing. People use nouns to make things more official; I think it's the idea of labelling processes that somehow makes us think we've done something more sophisticated or more impressive. So we don't say we've been *asking people something*,

over-reliance on nouns is a classic feature of business writing we say there has been a *consultation*. We don't ask people what they *need*, but instead what their *requirements* are. Or we talk about a *delivery strategy* rather than just *getting stuff done*.

The effect of this nominalisation (see, anyone can do this turning verbs into nouns lark) is again to remove what we write from the way that we would say it in person. In fact, using verbs a lot is one of the things that makes English distinctively English; French tends to favour nouns where we like verbs, and German typically knocks them together to form new concepts (indeed, the sign above could have pretty much been translated from one German word). Think back to *operational excellence* versus *doing everyday things better*. Just having a verb at the beginning of the second bit is making it feel more active and direct.

Use too many nouns in English then, and your writing feels dehumanised, bureaucratic, or just long-winded and confusing.

CHAPTER 9

One thing leads to another

How to put your words
together better

Active not passive

O nce you've started using more verbs (well done), you've still got a couple of choices as to how to use them. That's because there are two fundamental ways of constructing verbs in English. Introducing, ladies and gentlemen, the active voice and the passive voice. And which one you pick will make a big difference to the feel of your writing.

> there are two fundamental ways of constructing verbs in English

Now, the difference is quite a tricky thing to explain, so I'll do my best without turning this into the kind of hideous grammar lesson you remember from your childhood (or maybe you don't because you're part of the lost generation who never got taught it. I'm one, really; I learnt most of my grammar through learning other languages).

An active sentence is when the *subject* of your sentence (usually the person or the thing at the beginning of the sentence) is doing the action:

I go

You eat

Neil wrote a million-selling business book

We have decided

... and so on. A passive sentence is when the subject of the sentence has something done to them:

I am hit

You are told

Jon was sent to Coventry

We will be informed.

(The clue to spotting a passive is it usually has a bit of the verb *to be* lurking in there, like *am*, *was*, *been*, etc., although it's not always foolproof.) Now, lots of writers will tell you not to use the passive, for all kinds of (often spurious) reasons. But it is true that in conversation we use mostly active sentences, and hardly any passive. In writing, however, and particularly business writing, the number of passive sentences soars. That has the effect of removing the tone of your writing from something you would actually say, and, as I keep banging on about in this book, getting your writing to feel like something you could naturally say is often the key to business writing glory.

There are times where you would naturally use the passive in speech; and if you'd say it, it's fine to write it. So the question is, how do you get rid of those passive sentences you really don't need? The answer is usually to flip the sentences round. So if you've written (passively):

if you'd say it, it's fine to write it

I was told by Bill

ask yourself the question, who did the action? It was Bill. Bill told me. Not only is it more typically conversational, but you've saved yourself a few words, which is handy, too. It's not always this clear-cut who's doing the action, though. Take a sentence I mentioned in the previous chapter:

This will be implemented in June.

From that sentence, it's impossible to tell who's doing the action (it's why bureaucracies love the passive; it can leave a nice bit of ambiguous wiggle room about who's actually taking responsibility for things). In fact, people in workshops have confessed to me that they've used the passive when they've had to write about a decision they disagreed with (even if they were part of the group that made the decision). So, instead of saying:

We decided to make 100 people redundant

they wrote:

It was decided that 100 people would be made redundant.

The meaning is the same, but the writer has distanced him- or herself from the responsibility. That's why the passive can sometimes feel a tiny bit shifty and dishonest.

So, faced with a sentence like: *This will be implemented in June*, what do you do? Your choice is to either leave it passive, or do a bit of thinking (or a bit of digging) to find out who'll really be doing the implementing. So you might change that to: *The finance team will implement this in June* – if that's what's actually going to happen. You'll see that not only can this feel more direct, and not surprisingly, more, er, active, but you can make things more personal; active sentences are more likely to feature an *I* or a *we* or a *you* because that's what we'd

> active sentences are more likely to feature an *I* or a *we* or a *you*

naturally do in conversation. So, let's say you're talking to customers, you might change (two passives in this, by the way):

*Customers **will be informed** when their order is ready **to be collected***

to

***We**'ll tell you when **you** can collect your order*

– so third person (customers) becomes second person (you), which helps even more to imbue the sentence with warmth and naturalness.

The tools of the trade

If you've spotted that you're prone to overuse of the passive in your writing (which many of us are), clever versions of Microsoft Word will even underline it for you and point out the error of your ways. Like all computer-driven language stuff, it's not entirely reliable, so you sometimes have to take it with a pinch of salt, because speaking a language natively is happily so subtle and complicated and intuitive that computers are a long way from mastering it.

And if you like the helping hand that gives you, there's another wee tool you can use if you're enslaved to the corporate monster that is Microsoft. You'll find that you have an option in Word that'll give you a hand to monitor not only what percentage of your writing is made of passives, but more, too. In the options for spell check and grammar check, you can tick a box to 'show readability statistics'. Once that's done, when you do your spell and grammar check, at the end it will show you a box which gives you a score for how readable your writing is. It is rather grandly titled the Flesch Reading Ease test, and is based largely on the length of your sentences and the length of the words you're using. I've just checked the first draft of this book, and it scores a 70.0, and the higher the score, the better (unlike your passive percentage, where I scored 4 per cent. Phew!).

It also tells you what age of American schoolchild should be able to read your work. (That could also be pretty useful, if I had any idea what their grades correspond to in real money.) But your target should probably be surprisingly low. The *Economist* newspaper (well, they call themselves a newspaper but it looks like a magazine to me), apparently have in mind an eight-year-old child when they write; not in terms of the content (the economic ramifications of globalisation might be beyond even the most precocious eight-year-old), but in terms of the language in which it's written (or, the language they write it in, if you really want me to avoid all passives). It's this knack of getting their writing to sound clear enough for a child that gives the *Economist* its clout; people read its clarity as intelligence.

You talking to me?

> ### brilliant tip
>
> Questions give your writing more impact.

When was the last time you started a bit of writing with a question? Not recently, will be the answer most of us would give. But questions are a brilliant way of making your writing feel more engaging. Why? Because if you start with a question – especially one that's aimed directly at the reader – you get your reader thinking. Thinking, what's the answer to that question? Or, even better, what's *my* answer to that question? And if your readers are thinking, then they're not just letting the words wash over them. It's not just that, either. Questions have a number of benefits for your writing.

> if your readers are thinking, then they're not just letting the words wash over them

1   **They make you think from your reader's point of view**. We've seen that, too often when we write, we're just thinking about what we've got to say. That might be OK if that's interesting enough, but we might be much more fascinated about our particular subject than anyone else. Using a few questions forces you to put yourself in your reader's shoes. What are *they* really interested in? What do they absolutely need to know? Thinking of the questions your reader is thinking of will make what you're saying much more relevant to them. And if you don't just think of those questions, but write them down too, then your reader will be reassured that you've got their best interests at heart: 'Wow, that's exactly what I was wondering. This writer's really helpful.' That's why the FAQs (frequently asked questions) bit is usually the best written bit of any website. Only there do people really focus on their readers (or maybe they've learnt from bitter experience what people don't understand from reading the rest of the website). Of course, arguably, an FAQs page is an admission of failure. Your website shouldn't really need one. Probably the writer should just have thought at the beginning what the readers' FAQs were going to be, and written about those on the rest of the website.

     And while you're walking a mile in your readers' shoes, if you ask a question that really gets to the heart of what's going on in their head, especially if it acknowledges their doubts or cynicism (something like 'Why are we bothering to do this rebranding programme, anyway?'), it can also be really disarming. Your readers give you credit for recognising the reality of their situation, or feelings, and you get them a little bit on side.

2   **They get you writing more conversationally**. Questions are an essential part of the way we talk. You ask something, and you get a response. They're a natural part of dialogue.

So, as soon as you start writing in them, your mindset changes. Your writing becomes less one-way (the problem with lots of distant-feeling corporate writing),

> questions are an essential part of the way we talk

and more two-way. Of course, a cynic would say that this is a con; it's still only one person writing. And that's true, but questions are the closest you'll get to instilling that two-way sense into your writing without turning it into a script.

There's a saying, 'Ask a straight question, and get a straight answer.' Use questions well, and you can harness some of that sense of straightforwardness when you do come to answer the question you've posed. For instance, begin your answer to yes/no questions with one word – *yes*, or *no*:

Can I claim my prize over the internet?

Yes. Just go to our website, click on to 'competitions' and follow the instructions.

Of course, not all your questions will fall neatly into *yes/no*. But you can keep this feeling of directness in other ways. Think, how would I actually answer this question? Starting your answer with *Well*,... nearly always works. Even a *maybe* will make you feel straightforward, as long as you go on to explain why you can't be completely definitive.

3 **They make structure and navigation really clear**. As we saw right at the beginning, questions are also a cunning way of showing your reader how your document hangs together. After all, most of the things we write at work we must be writing to answer questions of some sort. So, if you make those questions abundantly clear, it makes your reader's life very easy indeed. Lots of writers struc-ture everything they ever write

> lots of writers structure everything they ever write through questions

through questions; they might not use the questions as headings in the final version, but they can help get your thinking clear about what the real point of each part of your document is supposed to be doing. Think of this book; you could see its different sections answering questions like:

Why does this book exist?

What should I do before I start?

How should I put it together?

What's the right style?

How do I make it really memorable?

As it happens, I haven't used those headings, but there's no reason why I couldn't have. And we've seen that, arguably, the journalist's trade is completely based on thinking about questions: who, what, when, where, why and how (it's such a shame that the last one doesn't start with *w*). And they get paid to write for a living every day. Keep thinking a little bit like one of them (not for too long, mind, lest you get too hardbitten and world-weary), and you'll probably do all right.

CHAPTER 10

What not to write

Some deadly writing sins

The 'as opposed to?' test

I hesitated to write this at the beginning of this book, for fear of putting some of you off, but, in truth, most business writing is about selling. Even if you're not literally selling something (which you might be if you're writing the side of a yoghurt pot, or a proposal to do some consultancy), then you might be selling your ideas, or your arguments. If you're writing a letter of complaint, then you're selling your reasons why you deserve your money back, or a case of champagne, or whatever it is you want to shut you up. If you're writing a CV, you're selling yourself.

> most business writing is about selling

The problem is that selling things is tricky, and if you're British, faintly embarrassing (our American cousins are much more able to deal with the horror of it all). Most people when they get into selling mode in their writing start using all manner of hyperbolic adjectives; just the sort of thing you see if you walk down the high street during the sales:

AMAZING SAVINGS!!

FANTASTIC DEALS!!

UNBEATABLE VALUE!!

When we're not selling stock, we do something similar, just with a different set of overeager words. When I work with professional services firms – people like lawyers, accountants, management consultants and the like – and they're touting for work, they nearly always use phrases like 'You'll be working with a dedicated team of expert consultants.' Nothing wrong with that, you might think. Nor the bit people write at the beginning of people's CVs when they write 'Neil is a conscientious team player, outgoing and excellent in a crisis.'

The problem with this sort of writing is that it leaves you thinking, 'Well, you would say that, wouldn't you?' You wouldn't expect someone at the beginning of their CV to write, 'To be honest, I'm OK at my job, but I get bored quite easily and on a bad day some of my colleagues drive me up the wall' (although I'd be pretty tempted to interview them if that landed on my desk, just because they sound like a real person). The fact that you *say* you're conscientious doesn't really count for very much. Just as when you walk down the high street and you see 'AMAZING SAVINGS', you don't expect to walk in, your eyes to widen, mouth to drop, and you to fall out of your shoes with astonishment at the £5 off a mediocre pair of trousers. We put these words in because they're what we want our readers to take out of our message. But just putting the words in doesn't make our readers believe it; we're more astute than that, and more suspicious of the spin people put on things.

> just putting the words in doesn't make our readers believe

In fact, they can have the opposite effect. Sometimes it can seem that you're trying so hard to convince your reader of something that it feels like you don't really believe it yourself. Introducing the *as opposed to?* test: a good way of checking if the words (especially adjectives) you're using are convincing, or even necessary. One of my clients writes letters to customers that say things like:

If your problem can't be resolved immediately, our highly skilled team will take ownership of managing it through to resolution.

Now, it might take a whole chapter to talk about all the things we could improve about that sentence. But let's concentrate on that *highly skilled team*. Ask yourself: as opposed to? Our woefully undertrained team? Clearly no one would ever write that; it's absurd. But if the opposite is so absurd, you probably don't need to put in the *highly skilled* at all. In fact, when people work on this sentence in my training sessions what they interpret from it is, 'We've had to pass this thing on to some people who at least vaguely know what they're doing, because the first lot had no idea.' Which may well be the case, but there's no need to put that thought into your customers' minds.

Or take the dedicated team of expert consultants. As opposed to? An uninterested team of amateur consultants? Exactly. These words aren't pulling their weight.

But enough about what's wrong with Hyperbolic Adjective Overload (I'm going to ™ that), what do you do about it? Well, the first step is just to take them out, and already it will sound better:

Our team will take ownership...

(OK, that *ownership* is still yucky but one step at a time, here), or

You'll be working with a team of consultants.

These versions already sound calmer and more confident, because they're trying much less hard to impress. They're less of the used-car salesman, and more of the seasoned pro who oozes credibility.

But of course, you might still want your reader to *feel* that the team is highly skilled, or the team of consultants is dedicated and expert, without having to say it. So we need to show, not tell. Here you've got two choices: prove it, or make it feel it.

1 **Prove it**. We're all much more likely to believe facts than vague assertions, like we're *skilled* or we're *dedicated*. So an easy way to get this message over is to note the proof of what you're saying. Is this team of consultants dedicated to me because they won't be working on any other projects? Or is it the fact that I can ring them at home on their mobiles 24 hours a day, if I'm sad enough to want to? What makes them expert? Have they got a PhD in exactly the thing they're doing for me? If any of these are the case, say so. It'll take a few more words, but be a hundred times more convincing:

> we're all much more likely to believe facts than vague assertions

> *You'll be working with a team of consultants. Every one of them has worked in mechanical engineering for over ten years, and for the length of this project they won't be working on anything else.*

2 **Make it feel it**. The second way to do it, which is admittedly harder, is to let the way you write, rather than what you write, convey the message. Think of a novel that starts:

> *He walked in. He could feel his heart beginning to race, so tried to breathe deeper. He failed. Something was coming; he couldn't see what, but the shadow loomed up along the hallway and was almost upon him.*

The next sentence of this piece should not be *It was exciting*, or *He was nervous*. That should be obvious, from the pace of the writing and the details within it. George Orwell's *Nineteen Eighty-Four* starts:

> *It was a bright, cold day in April, and the clocks were striking thirteen.*

And he doesn't need to add, *which was odd*. His reader knows it's odd, and, in fact, it feels odder that it's mentioned but not commented on or explained. And it's why Dan Brown's *Da Vinci Code*, although a gripping story, is horribly written. The first line is:

> *Renowned curator Jacques Saunière staggered through the vaulted archway of the museum's Grand Gallery.*

The very first word is a let-down. He's telling us about the character, rather than letting his character emerge through the things he does, or the things he says. Not only is it lazy, and mildly insulting to your reader, but it's less convincing. Just because the author *says* someone is renowned, why should we believe him? Much better to make the character *seem* renowned, either through his erudition, or the way other characters treat him, than just to say it. If we work it out for ourselves, we believe it more. It's often what readers mean when they say, 'I just didn't believe in the character of such-and-such.' What they mean is the author's description of that character just didn't seem plausible; we're told they were one thing but the writing didn't bear it out.

Dan Brown is telling, not showing. Your writing needs to do the latter, too. If you want something to sound exciting, write it in an exciting way. If you want something to seem important, make it feel important. And you'll be able to use some of the techniques that are coming up in the next chapter to do it.

> if you want something to seem important, make it feel important

Don't hedge

One of the things that stops a lot of people writing well is the fear that it could come back and bite them. Printed on paper, or stored on your computer, our worst fears are that somehow the words we write will be quoted back at us by a snarling barrister in a court of law twenty years hence. It will never, ever, happen to most of us, of course, but the fear is still there. The written word feels permanent in a way that what comes out of our mouth does not. In fact, people are just as likely to write down what you said and quote it back to you (employment tribunals are made of this), but nevertheless what we say feels more fleeting and insubstantial than what we write, instead being carried away on the air and frequently forgotten.

The effect of this is that it can make people really reluctant to commit themselves in writing. So you find business writing full of *we aim to*, *it is our intention to*, *it may be possible to*, *we are committed to*, *we are dedicated to*, and the like. Naturally this diminishes the power of what you're saying; it sounds like you want to say something of substance, but at the last minute you bottle it. Think of the effect if Churchill had said:

We aim to fight them on the beaches.

Or,

I may be able to offer you blood, toil, tears and sweat.

Think of the tenets of religious thought; commandments don't work too well if you pussy-foot around what you've got to say:

Thou shalt aim not to kill.

So, in the words of what I believe to be a George Michael song: if you've got something to say, why don't you say it? It'll make you sound more confident, more authoritative and more likely to do what you say you will.

But there's another reason why sometimes you should be happy to be really direct. Sometimes, it's the only honest thing to do. When things have gone wrong, if you try to cover them up, spinning and hedging your way into a slightly spuriously positive message, your reader usually spots it. And it gets their back up, because it sounds like you've not got the guts to acknowledge the reality of the situation. Tell the truth, and it's quite disarming for your reader. A couple of years ago I was taking the Tube in London the day after one of their occasional Really Bad Days. The manager of the line wrote a message to customers the next day, which was put up on posters in the stations that had been affected. The first line was:

> tell the truth, and it's quite disarming for your reader

> *I am sorry for the awful Tube journey that many of you had yesterday.*

I think it's a brilliant first line. It starts personally, with some real everyday language (*I am sorry* not *I apologise*, or even *Please accept Transport for London's apologies for any inconvenience that may have been caused*, which is what you're expecting to read in that situation). But the killer word is the word *awful*. It's a word which most of us wouldn't have had the guts to use in that situation, because, if we were the manager of that line, it highlights what a terrible job we've done. But actually, most people I've shown this poster to don't react negatively to the word *awful*, they react well. We admire the fact that he's told the truth about the situation; it's disarming. It makes him seem like a real person, and we empathise with him because of it.

It's bad news week

Here's an example that takes the same tactic even further, and it's from an annual report. Now, if any of you have ever read an annual report, you'll know they're pretty damn dull. And if you're the writer, they're a nightmare. They're written by committee, and they're the most highly scrutinised documents imaginable. That's because the chief executive is likely to be stressing about it because their bonus is on the line – or maybe his or her job is on the line – and if it's a corporate one, then it gets sent to analysts in the City who are poring over it to see if they can spot where the company has had some unforgivable strategic mishap, or where they're massaging the truth to cover up what has gone wrong.

And if these reports are tricky to write in a good year, in a bad year they're even worse. There was even a bit of research that proved that, on average, annual reports are twice as long in a bad year as in a good one. That's because they start doing many of the things I've been arguing against in this book. Their words get longer and more abstract, their sentences longer and more complex. They hedge what they're saying in an attempt to justify themselves, and it comes out feeling woolly and vague. So, this example is from Ericsson's annual report in 2002, and they'd had a shocker. They'd got just about everything wrong that they could get wrong. In fact, they'd done so badly, they'd made the largest loss in Swedish corporate history. They had to write the first page of this report, and address what happened, without sending their investors into panic and straight into their brokers to sell their shares.

This is what they wrote:

> *2002 was tough. Our customers bought less equipment, the rollout of 3G was slow, and the market was hard to predict. Some observers see no end to these difficulties. We take a very different view.*

I don't know about you, but it convinces me. It works because it's not scared to talk about the things that went wrong – the negative stuff. Admittedly, it doesn't completely take responsibility for them (it says *the customers bought less equipment* rather than *we sold less equipment* which would be arguably more honest), but nevertheless it doesn't gloss over things, either. This is particularly effective here because most people reading these words would already have some idea of the hopeless state of the market that year. So, having the courage to own up to the things that the reader has in their head pays off, because you tackle the very worst thing that they think they could throw at you.

No hedging; no excuses. Just bags of confidence. You get it out of the way quickly, and get the chance to move on, and the report feels like it's refreshingly honest and in touch. It's a win–win.

Word limits

> **brilliant** tip
>
> Set yourself a limit if it makes your writing more succinct.

A lot of people tell me their writing problem is being long-winded. They start writing, and then just go on. And on. And on. And that's a problem if we're being pessimistic about our readers, because by now we know the longer we're writing, the fewer people are reading what we have to say.

There are a few reasons why we write too much. First, we might be thinking too much about what we've got to say, rather than what our reader is really bothered about. You might have been working on a project for three months, but you don't need to tell me exactly what you did every single day if the real point is that you successfully built an airport.

Second, sometimes we're scared about leaving out an important detail. But actually, our readers are pretty tolerant of this; in most situations we have more of a relationship with our readers than just one document. If there's something else that's crucial that they need to know, which you haven't told them, they can usually e-mail you, or ring your call centre, or look at your website. In fact, that can be quite a trick, because sometimes the aim of your writing will be to develop a deeper relationship with your reader, so it might be good to leave them wanting a little more: you might get to talk to them again. Remember The Writer's little book of writing rules? It promises *The 10 secret rules of business writing*, but in the book there are only seven. The book says, 'we'll tell you the other three when you ring us', so we then get a chance to use our devastating wit and charm in person to turn a casual reader into someone who knows us a bit, and starts to feel warm towards us.

> it might be good to leave them wanting a little more

Another reason for verbal diarrhoea is that sometimes, as we've seen, we're thinking as we write. We start off in one direction, but distract ourselves and start heading off on a different tack before, if we're lucky, heading back to the main point. Now unless you're a rambling but raffish raconteur of the highest order, that's likely just to annoy your reader.

The final reason is that it's just plain easier to write something long than it is to write short. Because you're not worrying about what your reader's thinking, and not planning what you're going to say, you can just dive in and do it and get it over with quicker. Not only does it take less thinking, it takes less courage. You need guts to leave things out. There's a quotation about exactly this which is usually attributed to Churchill but is also put down to pretty much any clever person who's ever lived – Cicero, Descartes, it could have been any of them. Whoever it was, they hit the nail on the head:

> *I'm sorry I wrote you such a long letter; I didn't have time to write a short one.*

So what do you do about it if you try to do all the things above and you realise you're still, by your very nature, a waffler?

Well, maybe you need to set yourself some rules. Instead of letting yourself ramble, get strict. Word limits are the most obvious way to do it. When I've worked with people who are writing papers to present to the boards of their organisations, a word limit has made all the difference. Now these limits are usually pretty arbitrary. 'Make your recommendation in 100 words.' Even 'Summarise the point of this proposal in 12 words or fewer.' There's nothing magical about 12 or 100 words. But any limit at all (as long as it's a fair bit less than you would normally write in a given situation) can transform the way people write.

> instead of letting yourself ramble, get strict

An experiment, in summary

In workshops, I sometimes ask people to summarise an article from the *Economist* in twelve words or fewer. I usually find an article that's a fairly chunky few paragraphs long, so it's not easy. Most people find it difficult, and people always do it in different ways, but even the most hardened ramblers usually get there in the end. When they've done that, I then take the word limit away, and ask them to write a second version, this time including anything they felt really bad about cutting out the first time. And then two spooky things happen.

About half the room really struggles. They don't quite understand it, given that they found it difficult with the word limit, so you'd think taking away the constraint would make their lives much easier. But what they say is that having *really* got to the point the first time round, they don't want to lose the beautiful efficiency of the first version. They're happy with where they got to.

The other half of the room feels much happier, revelling in the chance to use a few more words and mention absolutely everything they think is important. And then, when I get them to read their new versions out, they usually realise that they've gone back to waffling again, that their first versions were better, and that they could cut a lot of what they've just added back in.

Start at the end

What does this experiment prove? Well, maybe a bit of discipline is good for all of us. When you've got to something clear and focused, why would you then want to go back and muddy the waters? It's for this reason that lots of writers, myself included, when faced with the prospect of writing something long, start with the summary. It's a counter-intuitive place to start, because we've been trained to do the summary once everything else is in place. But writing the summary first helps you to be super-clear about what you're going to say, and what's important and what's not. It means that when you go on to write the rest of the document, you're much more critical about what you need to include and what you don't. It makes the writing as a whole much tighter. Heck, once I've written a good summary, sometimes I realise there's just no point writing the long version. The writer Elmore Leonard says, 'Leave out the parts readers tend to skip.' And who can argue with that?

CHAPTER 11

Mythbusting

The things we were told
that are wrong but are
right

OK, I've said a few times in this book that schools have a lot to answer for. The things we're taught at school can stay absolutely etched into our heads for the rest of our lives, and sometimes I feel like I spend most of my career unpicking some of these things.

Not that teachers teach these things out of mischief. I'm sure they all want their wards to get on in life, and think that some grumpy employer somewhere is going to see them split an infinitive and write them off as a dunderhead. But lots of the things we were taught were grammatical rules are nothing more than old wives' tales, promulgated by people who don't know very much about language or its history. Just because you can talk or write doesn't mean you know anything much about how language actually works. As linguists Laurie Baher and Peter Trudgill point out, even if you're *very* good at breathing it doesn't make you an expert in respiratory biology.

So here are a few bits of linguistic nonsense that need to be done away with forever. And you can take it from me, because I've got a degree in linguistics and everything.

You can start a sentence with *and*

 **tip**

Use *and*, and *but* etc. in sentences where you would naturally do so in speech.

You really can start a sentence with 'and'. And *but*.

Or *or*.

So that mean's *so* is fine, too.

But not too often.

You get the point. Most people were taught at school that these words were banned because they're 'conjunctions', and you can't start a sentence with a conjunction (no explanation why, you notice, just can't). If people are really struggling to defend this rubbish, they say it's 'illogical' or it doesn't make sense. It can't be that illogical because most of us do it in speech a hundred times a day, and no one bats an eyelid. No-one has ever stopped me and said 'Hold on there, pal. You just started a sentence with *and*, you illogical freak.' The fact is yes, these words sometimes join two bits of a sentence, but not always. Sometimes they connect thoughts, but across sentences. As I write this book there's a great poster campaign by the charity Stonewall that says, 'Some people are gay. Get over it.' We need to do the same about *and* and *but*; just get over it. And anyway (see, there I go again), *however* does pretty much the same thing as *but*, and *therefore* pretty much the same as *so*, yet they seem to be allowed at the beginning of a sentence, just because they're longer and supposedly cleverer. You see: nonsense.

Again, the point is, if it feels natural, if it sounds right, you can do it. *And, but* and *so* will give you a really nice conversational feel to your writing. *And* is especially useful at the end of a paragraph, to give the rhythm a satisfying bit of finality:

> if it feels natural, if it sounds right, you can do it

We're going to do this.

We're going to do this.

And we're going to do the other.

See? Satisfying, isn't it? Occasionally, people's grammar checkers on their computers will wade into the debate and tell them you're not allowed to do this. Ignore them; remember, you can walk into Starbucks and order a short skinny mochaccino and your computer can't. They can't be that clever.

 **brilliant** tip

Use contractions when you want your writing to have a conversational feel.

There's no such word as *can't*

Another thing which is patently ridiculous. For a word that doesn't exist (presumably *don't* and *won't* and *shouldn't* don't exist either), it makes a suspiciously high number of appearances in everyday speech. If it were on the Witness Protection Programme it would have been easily spotted by the villains it snitched on and bundled off into a canal somewhere pretty damn sharpish.

Of course it exists. What the objectors (possibly conscientious, but not very bright) mean, of course, is that it's something that has traditionally been associated with speech and not writing.

there's no logical reason why cannot is right, and can't is wrong

Which is true, but business writing is changing, as we've seen. There's no logical reason why *cannot* is right, and *can't* is wrong. Some people claim *can't* is 'lazier' – presumably because it has fewer letters. But does that mean *opus* is lazier than *work of art*? That's not how language works. The point is, these words have different effects on your reader.

Because *can't* and *won't* and so on are the words we naturally use more often in speech, they will sound more human, and more natural. *Cannot* and *will not* feel more formal and more unarguable. If you write in an e-mail 'I can't do it because I don't have the time,' you sound natural, reasonable, if a little bit stressed. If you write 'I cannot do it because I do not have the time,' you sound much more unapproachable, like you're about to biff me in the eye if I make any more unreasonable demands about your workload.

So as a business writer, my default mode is *can't* and *won't* and the like because I'm usually trying to make my writing feel as natural and everyday as possible. I will use *cannot* and so on for deliberate effect, every now and again, to make my reader slow down, and make me seem more definitive:

We don't use materials that can't be recycled.

We don't import raw materials if we can get them locally.

And we do not use child labour, or pay people an unreasonable amount for their hard work. Ever.

so forget the dogma; pick the one that sounds right

But it's all about effect. There is no logical grammatical argument here. So forget the dogma; pick the one that sounds right in your sentence.

brilliant tip

Use the everyday words you use in conversation.

There's no such word as *get*

This is another load of old cobblers. Loads of people were told at school not to write the word *get*. Why? Well, there was rarely an actual reason, just the line 'It's not a word that you write' (which is just too circular to be an argument). The main objection to words like *get* is that it's common. And it is common, in a statistical sense, in that it's very frequent in everyday language. Partly, that's because it's an incredibly versatile word. It turns up in all kinds of different contexts, which is why its entry in the full *Oxford English Dictionary* is pages long. That's why it has tons of synonyms; it can mean the same thing as:

receive

gain

obtain

become

and all manner of other words. But it's common-ness – in the sense of frequency – seems, in the minds of some linguistic nutters, to have become translated into a kind of social commonness; because it's so everyday it's seen as somehow unsophisticated. This is nothing more than barely disguised snobbism. After all, *the* is a very common word in the English language, but no one argues that because of that you should try to use something else instead; it would be nonsense. Certain words are common not because people are unimaginative, but because these words are really useful, and occasionally, essential to get your point across.

The result of this spurious rule is that people contort their sentences into all kinds of gymnastically uncomfortable turns of phrase to avoid saying it. People write, 'when I received your e-mail', or 'I have gained experience in a butcher's and gained an NVQ in basic-level calf-slicing.' In both of those cases, if you were talking, you'd naturally use *get*: 'when I got your e-mail'; 'I got experience in a butcher's and an NVQ,' and to my ears at least, both of those sentences sound perfectly fine, because they feel absolutely natural. In fact, I'd argue that 'I have gained experience' sounds really quite pompous, because the writer is trying so damned hard to avoid the word which is completely instinctive in that context.

So if you mean *get*, say *get*. Try it, it's strangely liberating. And it's allowed. We're all grown-ups; we can have our pudding before our main course if we really want, too. Writing in this style, with words we'd naturally say but don't often write, can even give a little touch of magic. Which is what Part Four's all about.

CHAPTER 12

Sound advice

Why some words just
sound right

Magic words

keep banging on about how we should all try to write more like we speak, because it sounds sincere and natural. And that there are certain words that are bound to get in the way of that estimable mission. Words like *ensure*, which we write but never say (people protest that they do, but only if they're being influenced by their writing. You've never said in a million years 'Oh, by the way, darling, if you're going to the shops later, can you ensure that you pick up a pint of milk?' Or 'Can you find out what little Wayne's kit requirements are for scout camp?'). These all fail another brilliant test that Elmore Leonard set of his own writing. He says:

If it sounds like writing, I rewrite it.

Well, just as there are words that get my goat because they always sound false, there are also magic words that make your writing sound conversational because we say them a lot and hardly ever write them. The two that seem to come up most often are *really* and *so*.

We've already seen that *so* is the everyday translation for legalistic words like *thus* and *therefore*. Because people are still a wee bit shy of using words like *so* in their writing, it can do something really special for your writing. It instantly gives your writing the ring of authenticity, because it immediately reminds us of the spoken language, rather than the written. The word that does this best, for me, is the word *really*. Few of us write *really* very often. We've been trained instead to write words like *significantly* or *extremely*. But we say *really* all the time, and when you write it, it sounds like you really mean it (there you go). Compare

I'm extremely sorry that you are not happy with our service

and

I'm really sorry you're unhappy with our service.

You'd think *extremely* would be the most sorry-sounding, because it's so, well, extreme. But for me, the *really* is much more convincing. It has the ring of a real person; the ring of truth.

And that's magic.

Reading aloud allowed

 **brilliant** tip

Check what you write by reading it aloud.

In fact, reading aloud is pretty much essential. Because I keep rattling on about using the words that you'd really say, almost the most useful thing you can do to test if your writing is working or not is to read it out. Out loud, if possible, but if you work in an open-plan office and that feels just a wee bit

> reading aloud is positively encouraged

too embarrassing, you can train yourself to do the same thing in your head. After all, that's what your reader will be doing, too.

If you don't believe me that the sound of things is important, try this little test. Ask a few people what their favourite word is. Someone more numerate than me will be able to suggest what a statistically relevant sample would be for this experiment, but you probably need around ten. When you've asked them what their favourite word is, ask them why. What you'll find is that a few people will pick a word because they like what it represents. When we ask this in workshops, we get a lot of *shopping, weekend, holiday, chocolate* and the occasional *parachute* that tells us what that person likes doing with their time.

But more often, people don't talk about the meaning. Instead they talk about something a little more intangible, and often more emotive. Usually that means the sound of a word, or the associations of it. The ones that come up a lot in this category are *moist, serendipity, discombobulate* and *onomatopoeia* (or if you're a Kid Creole and the Coconuts fan, *Ona! Ona! Onomatopoeia!*). People talk about the rhythm of them, or the

> when we're writing at work, we're often in the wrong mode

way they feel in their mouth, or the shape it makes their face make. What this tells me is that when we're writing at work, we're often in the wrong mode.

Usually we're thinking about the content of our writing – the messages we have to get across. Indeed it's the message that we usually get feedback on, or that gets negotiated when other people's opinions get brought into the pot. But the favourite-word test says it's not just the content that our readers are responding to – in fact, it might not even be the content that they're mostly responding to – but it's also the sound and feel of our writing. I've run quite a lot of workshops at the BBC, and broadcasters are naturally aware of the power of words when they're spoken. When I'm there, the favourite words are even more dramatically skewed towards the things that people like the sound of. And you'll only be able to tune into this effect if you read your writing out.

Following the clues

Why is reading out so useful? Well, mainly because it gives you big clues as to how your writing is working. It might give you really simple clues. Try reading out a sentence that goes on without any commas but which keeps going beating around the bush and hedging its bets and not really getting to the point and pretty soon you'll find it gets increasingly difficult to breathe and you'll maybe begin to worry that you could die reading what someone's telling you about why they've missed their sales targets. That's telling you that your sentence is too long, and that you need to do something about it. What could you do? Well, the most obvious thing to do would be to break your sentence up into two or three smaller ones. Or maybe it needs some different punctuation.

Now, a lot of people are scared of punctuation, largely because ranting reactionaries like Lynn Truss and John Humphrys have written books pretty much telling us that we're moral weaklings if we can't get our punctuation right. (Truss might have her tongue in her cheek, but she really does say that. And even if she is joking, the same sentiment does seem to be lurking somewhere beneath lots of what she says.) Well, you're not. For one thing the rules of punctuation are arbitrary and a bit random; I mean why does *Neil's book* or *Lynn's madness* have an *'s*, but the *its* in *the dog and its kennel* doesn't? It's not exactly logical.

Acting up

Luckily, reading out loud can really help you some way through this minefield, in particular where to put full stops and commas. The important thing to remember here is that punctuation was invented for actors, to tell them where to breathe when they were looking at a script. Keep that in your head, and you can't go very far wrong, really.

> punctuation was invented for actors

If you want your reader to take a little pause, give them a comma. If you want a longer, more dramatic pause, it's a full stop. (There's a real trend in journalism to write single words with a full stop after each one, to force your reader to slow down and give each word massive emphasis. I'm. Not. Kidding.) Do you want them to read something like a question? Give them a question mark. And hardly ever do this! (I'll explain why exclamation marks get my goat in the next bit.)

Because you're thinking of your writing as a script, reading it out will tell you what you need to know in a way that just looking at it won't. A four-line sentence might look OK on the page, but as soon as you say it out loud, you'll find yourself in respiratory problems pretty sharpish. Leave the punctuation out, or put it in the wrong place, and your reader is forced to breathe in the wrong places, and the sense and the effect of what you're trying to say get lost.

But breathing and sentence length are the easy bit, really. Reading out will give you more subtle clues than that. Occasionally, when I get people to read things out in my workshops, funny things happen to their voices. And it means I can tell how they're feeling about their writing, sometimes even before they do.

What sort of things happen? Well, sometimes people trail off at the end of their sentences. Their voice gets quieter, there's less variation in its pitch, and they start to gabble. That tells me they're bored by what they're writing, so much so that they can't even be bothered to form the words properly. And if they're bored by what they've written – and they wrote it – then there's no hope for the reader. If you can't be bothered to read something out, they won't be bothered to read it either, even in their heads.

More trouble with lists

This boring voice particularly appears when people are dealing with lists. Lists are usually, by their nature, pretty boring. So if you get more than two or three things listed in a sentence – especially if each thing in the list is made up of a few long words – it becomes incredibly difficult to sustain your attention and your interest. We've already seen that the way to sort out a long list is to bullet point it. Then, if it *is* boring, at least people can see there's a list coming and skip it, if that's what they want to do.

People also get bored when the rhythm of what they've written on the page is too predictable. Again, this is something you won't see on the page, but will probably hear when you start to read it. Here's what happens with most boring business writing.

Typically, when we're writing at work we write a sentence which goes on for roughly the length of this sentence that I'm writing here (24 words). Then we follow that up with another sentence that goes on for almost exactly the same length as the one that went before it (24 words). You start to get hypnotised by the rhythm of these sentences one after another and you stop taking in the contents of each one (24 words). If you've got anything interesting to say in the fourth sentence, you can bet no one's listening because the monotonous rhythm is drilling into your head (25 words). If I start a fifth one you'll be getting aggravated enough to throw this book across the room and start looking for something else to do (26 words).

The solution? Well don't just go short all the time instead. That gets annoying, too. A bit staccato. Lacks flow. See? Instead, you need to introduce some variety in the length of sentences that you write. If you feel like you've gone on a bit, stop. Break the rhythm. If you're getting too short and punchy, stretch your legs a bit with a slightly longer

> introduce some variety in the length of sentences that you write

one. Get this variety right, and you'll find you'll be able to read it out in a much more interesting way, and as a result your reader will keep reading for longer.

The radio advertising voice

Sometimes people *can* be bothered to read the words out, but not in their normal voices. In fact, sometimes their delivery becomes really exaggerated. Usually that happens when people don't believe what they're writing, or have written it in a way that doesn't come naturally to them. Because they're not being true to themselves, when they read it out they can't read it as themselves. Instead, they have to take on a bit of a role; like an actor, they take on the character of someone who *would* write those words. This could be a 'techy' voice, or an official voice. But typically this happens when people are trying to sell things. They write things like

This is a fantastic opportunity, at an unbeatable price.

Usually to attempt to pull off a sentence like that, people put on what I call their radio advertising voice. Exaggeratedly enthusiastic and not very believable. Exclamation marks force people into this voice, too. The sentence above becomes even more incredible as

This is a fantastic opportunity, at an unbeatable price!

That's because the exclamation mark is there to make this thing (that the writer already doesn't believe) sound more exciting (when they're not genuinely excited about it). And our readers can pick up on that lack of confidence. In these days of corporate messages being over-hyped and over-spun, it sounds false. The key to finding out if you've got the tone right is to keep reading what you've written out. If you can read it out and still sound like you, you've got it. If there's a squirm in your voice, you need to go back and hone it until you've got something that feels more authentic.

> if you can read it out and still sound like you, you've got it

All this reading out means writing is a noisier profession than people sometimes give it credit for. And if you can't read it out loud, you have to train yourself to do it in your head. As I write this, I'm sitting on a train going to see my mum, and I'm having to mouth the words to myself as innocently as I can, so I don't look too deranged. Perhaps that's why so many writers have to work on their own; if they had to do all of this business in public, they might just look a little bit nuts.

PART 4

Magic

CHAPTER 13

A spoonful of sugar

Or how to bring your
writing to life

One of the principles of this book is that there's no need for anything you write to be boring. Ever. After all, boring writing doesn't get read (or at the very least, is only skim-read). And if no one reads it you might as well not have written it. It's a waste of your time. So all truly boring writing fails.

> there's no need for anything you write to be boring

Yet too often, we give ourselves that excuse. We say because we're writing IT policy, or about pensions, or the future of the sewage plant industry, it's bound to be boring. But that's not good enough. As the writer, it's your job to make it interesting. I often think of this in terms of rewarding your reader; after all, they're rarely under any obligation to read what you've got to say. So how do you thank them for sticking with you? Well, for most of us, it doesn't take much; we'll accept pretty paltry rewards. It's like the old HR adage that if you put £100 in most people's pay packets, they don't really notice. But if you spend £100 sending them and their partner out for a slap-up dinner, they remember it for yonks and are full of goodwill. Writing can be the same, so this chapter is all about the linguistic techniques for paying your reader back.

And if you *are* faced with really unpromising material, it might only be the way you write things that brings it to life. This is when the good business writer really earns their money, making a silk purse out of the proverbial sow's ear. So, assuming you've got your content sorted, and your structure decided, and you've got a fairly natural tone, how do you add a bit of oomph?

Telling tales

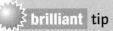 **brilliant** tip

Storytelling techniques will keep your reader reading for longer.

Are you sitting comfortably? Then I'll begin.

We've been telling each other stories for thousands of years. We get told them as children, and they stay with us for the rest of our lives, whether it's in the form of highbrow novels, soap operas on the telly, or big blockbuster movies. Nearly all of us seem to get the bug, and even if our tastes change, we never really seem to lose interest in the form itself.

And stories can be pretty sophisticated, too. Think of mythology, of any culture. It's been around for a long time, and it's more than just what happens to whom and where. Most mythology is based on the trials and tribulations of various characters (usually gods and beasts) but they nearly always have fairly weighty sub-texts: why the sun rises, how to keep your crops growing over a generation, or what is the true nature of love. It's clear that we don't just tell each other stories to keep each other amused; we use stories to explain things to ourselves and understand the world in a way beyond just what we can report through empirical evidence, the testimonies of our eyes and ears.

What's all this got to do with business writing? Well, if stories are so universal, and so ingrained in each of us, and so effective, it's surprising that businesspeople don't use them more to help get their messages across. And no surprise that really successful businesspeople often do communicate their ideas through the stories they come up with.

Take Innocent smoothies, a brand which came out of nowhere about over ten years ago, and absolutely took their market by storm (and are still growing four times faster than any of their competitors). I won't go on, because they've been written about by greater brains than me. But if you go to their website, in their equivalent of the 'about us' page, you'll even find a bit of writing headed 'our story':

> *In the summer of 1998 when we had developed our first smoothie recipes but were still nervous about giving up our proper jobs, we bought £500 worth of fruit, turned it into smoothies and sold them from a stall at a little music festival in London. We put up a big sign saying 'Do you think we should give up our jobs to make these smoothies?' and put out a bin saying 'YES' and a bin saying 'NO' and asked people to put the empty bottle in the right bin. At the end of the weekend the 'YES' bin was full so we went in the next day and resigned.*

You don't get a corporate vision, mission, values, brand essence, or onion, or dartboard or whatever other lunatic model is in fashion this week for helping people explain what they do. You get a short, simple story. A testament to its value is that when people mention Innocent in my workshops (which they do, frequently), people often quote this story back to me. How many 'about us' pages have you ever heard anyone quote, almost verbatim? It gets over their ethos, and it makes it memorable, by giving their corporate history a connection to real people, and a sense of place and time; it tells of a simple experiment that seemed to capture the spirit of their approach.

A boardroom story

Likewise, one of the biggest hits in the corporate publishing world in the last twenty years is the book *Who Moved My Cheese?* Its point is about people's attitude to change, but the star characters are two mice (admittedly, there are a couple of people in there, too). Now, most of the time we think of businesspeople as serious and stuffy. Not us, of course, only other businesspeople. But if the corporate textbook they all want to read is told through mice and cheese, that's got to be telling us something.

And sometimes, stories are the bread and butter of how businesses communicate with one another. Well, things that are supposed to be stories anyway. Go to lots of business-to-business websites, and you'll be confronted with 'case studies', where companies and organisations explain how they've helped out other companies and organisations. These are, to all intents and purposes, supposed to be stories. Yet usually, they're like watching paint dry. They're written to a formula, and all end up sounding exactly the same. Unless you happen to be insanely interested in the technical details of how one project might have differed from another, you'd probably never read more than two.

> sometimes, stories are the bread and butter of how businesses communicate with one another

Yet there's so much potential in a good case study. There are usually real characters, problems to be overcome, and enormous celebration (in a business style) if things end up going the right way. All the stuff of great narratives. But too often, we don't allow ourselves to have fun with those elements. Yet if we did, our readers would probably thank us.

But what is a story?

Well, at school we were taught that it's something with a beginning, middle and end. And there have been reams of debate written about this by people much more qualified than me on this subject. Scour the internet, and you'll find tons of different ideas. But here's one I like:

Someone... (a character)

Wants... (a quest, goal, mission)

But... (a challenge, quandary, interference)

So... (a means of succeeding, overcoming, finding)

Simple, eh?

Of course, a character can be a company, or a client, or whoever. But the key here is that when you transpose these structures to a business situation, you shouldn't drain all the life out of it. The character, if it is a company, still has to have the elements that make a character interesting: motivation, emotions and personality. Likewise, what they want might be something hard like a twenty per cent increase in sales, but a good story will explain why, or what's difficult about that, or how everyone would feel if that was achieved.

Look at the Innocent story in this light:

Someone... the boys behind Innocent

Want... to leave their current jobs and start a new company

But... they're nervous about it

So... they come up with an experiment to see if the public would support them.

it's that human element that brings the story to life

Note that the second and third lines are quite emotional; they're things we'd all identify with. And it's that human element that brings the story to life, and it's the bit that's woefully lacking from much business writing. But that doesn't just to have to come through in stories; there are other ways to do it, too.

Don't be backward in coming forward

brilliant tip

Say what you've got to say in the strongest terms.

I used to work with someone who never expressed an opinion on anything. It used to drive me nuts, because conversations would be pretty predictable. I'd make a point, and then he'd sort of agree with it, but then immediately half-heartedly put the opposite case, so that there was never any conclusion. Now, these are valuable skills if you're a diplomat, or maybe even a marriage guidance counsellor. As a brand consultant (which is what we were both doing at the time), it's a fairly fatal flaw. If you don't say what you think – even when you've sensibly weighed up both sides of an argument – then there's not really any point in consulting you. You'll just tell me what I already know. I found myself saying more and more extreme and incredible things just to see if I could get him to say that he really strongly disagreed with me. It was an uphill struggle, even when I was straight-facedly proposing the drowning in a canal of anyone who listens to U2.

Not surprisingly, he was a pretty boring writer, too, because his writing never really went anywhere. It had nothing to say; it felt wishy-washy and nondescript. Which, for the most part, is going to make your reader give up.

More journalistic thinking

Think of the people whose articles you like to read in the newspaper. Most people, when asked about that, can name a particular columnist or two. And in workshops, when I ask, people usually say that they like those columnists because they have strong, interesting opinions and they express them in a lively way. It certainly isn't that people just like the columnists they agree with, either. Write with enough flair, and even people who vehemently oppose what you've got to say will still find the expression of your ideas engaging. I used to love reading Julie Burchill's columns in the *Guardian*. Sometimes her urban lefty values chimed with my own, but just as often I found myself throwing the paper down, saying 'What on *Earth* are you talking about, you deliberately provocative, mad old crone?' But I still read what she had to say every week. The same is true in business.

Timidity is usually fairly tedious, while a clear statement of opinion invites people to engage with what you've got to say, one way or another. The Body Shop has built a brand pretty much based on a set of opinions, notably:

> a clear statement of opinion invites people to engage with what you've got to say

AGAINST ANIMAL TESTING

Not only does it encourage people to read what you have to say, it suggests that because there are things you feel strongly about, business for you is not just about making money. It's about doing things a certain way, with a certain set of principles. And whether people agree with those principles or not, the fact that you have them will make you seem more like a group of real businesspeople than a mere corporation. And as I keep saying in this book, we're much more interested in what real people have to say than what a faceless organisation thinks.

When we were asked to write an article for the *Financial Times* a little while ago, we decided to make it a very opinionated opinion piece, to make as sure as we could be that it would actually get read. So we decided to make our own pitch by attacking the authors of some of the main planks of prevailing linguistic wisdom of the day (yep, I'm talking about the dreaded Truss and Humphrys again). It was written by our managing director, Martin Hennessey:

> *I'm getting a bit miffed with these nanny-ish proclamations about punctuation. It's not that the use of jargon is good (obviously it isn't). Nor that that apostrophe shouldn't be wielded correctly (it should). It's the nagging that rankles. I blame the idea that 'plain' English is something to be aspired to in business. Who wants to be plain in life? No professional writer I know.*

Of course, to have an opinion, you don't just have to be attacking something (although using the power of negative emotion is something that we'll come back to). You can of course express something positive; it's just important that you express *something*.

I was working with a group the other day from the Pension Protection Fund in the UK, who step in if a company goes bust and all its former employees need their pensions paying. Like most organisations, they have at least two internal boards who you might have to write to if you work there. You might write to ask them for money for a particular project, or to get them to approve your decision to start doing something and stop doing something else.

I work with lots of people who have to write for boards like this, and it can be pretty nerve-wracking. Often you're writing to people you've never even met, who might be older and more senior than you. If you're arguing that they should keep funding your team, or your project, you might even be trying to persuade them that you have a future in your business or organisation. So our instinct, especially if we're British, is to be a bit deferential; we lay out the facts of our project or our case, and hope that with a bit of gentle nudging, they'll head towards the right conclusion.

Only it doesn't often work like that. Have a think about those people on that board. They're busy. Even busier than you, probably, and you're pretty busy. And they might not even be experts in the subject you're asking them to make decisions about; after all, many people hold positions on the boards of all kinds of different organisations. They're often employed for their intelligence and experience, rather than their specific expert knowledge.

I work with the board of another organisation who have board meetings on a Monday morning. But they don't get the papers for that meeting until Friday afternoon, and there might be up to twenty papers, all fighting for their attention, and all incredibly long and quite wishy-washily diplomatic and deferential. Now, when are those board members supposed to read those papers? Well, the only chance they've got is to do it is over the weekend, when there's that church fête on and *Doctor Who* is on the telly. So it's no surprise then they kept saying that they just wanted those documents to be shorter, and clearer about what they were saying. They've rewritten the document templates to make it clear what they want. The first sub-heading is *Recommendation*. So the first thing they want on that bit of paper is the writer's opinion.

And Partha Dasgupta, the former chief executive of the Pension Protection Fund, said exactly the same thing when he came to our workshop: put everything you've got to say in two pages max, and tell me what you're recommending (that is, your opinion), before you say anything else.

Think negative

brilliant tip

Don't be afraid to talk about negative things, if it makes your message more powerful.

A lot of people, especially those who work in HR or marketing, have been trained always to look for the positive in what they write, with the idea that if you write positively, then your reader will think positively of you or the business. And in many situations, that's going to be true. But there are certain times when a bit of negativity will actually give your writing a bit of welly. And sometimes it will be dangerous to be too positive.

> sometimes it will be dangerous to be too positive

So, when might you want to accentuate the negative? Well, I've said stories are important and some people argue that nearly every great story is rooted in conflict. The conflict between Romeo's family and Juliet's; between David and Goliath; heck, even between Bridget Jones and her men, society's expectations and her own impulses. Yes, it might be that that conflict is resolved at the end of the story, but you need the conflict to introduce drama, tension and emotion, all the things that we respond to in a story (remember that the third line of that story structure starts with 'but'; it's forcing you to introduce a negative element, or at least a little doubt). So, if you studiously avoid the negative all the time, you're missing a chance to get your reader engaged.

In workshops, when people are trying to tell us about their company, we often ask people to imagine what the commandments of their company religion would be. We ask them for some positive stuff – like what are the things everyone in the company believes in – but we also ask: what are you fighting against? It's often that question that elicits the most interesting answers, because you unearth some real passion. People come up with all kinds of answers:

Wasteful uses of energy

Mediocre design

Loan sharks who are out to exploit vulnerable people

Boring chocolate

If you can take this material and write about it in an interesting way, you've got the beginnings of a really passionate bit of writing. Indeed, some companies have made their whole ethos about supposedly negative thoughts. When Nike set up shop in the 1960s, their mission was to 'smash Adidas'. And as we've just seen, The Body Shop have built a brand that's all about what they are against. I've noticed that since L'Oréal have taken over The Body Shop, 'AGAINST ANIMAL TESTING' has become much less prominent in their communications. They're starting to display the typical corporate reticence to exploit a negative thought. They've changed the emphasis to focus on ideas like 'Love Your Body', and for me they sound less confident and less clearly different to their competition as a result.

> some companies have made their whole ethos about supposedly negative thoughts

… and the clocks were striking thirteen

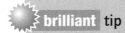

brilliant tip

Start with an arresting first sentence.

Which bit of your writing should you be thinking hardest about? The beginning, of course. The start of your writing is when your reader is thinking about whether what you've got to say is relevant, or interesting, or entertaining, or, in short, in any way worth a few minutes of their valuable time.

It's something that writers of fiction know instinctively – and something which we mere mortals know when we're in a more storytelling frame of mind. In our training sessions, we often get people to write the first paragraphs of a novel, one they've probably never read but been briefly briefed on by someone else who's in the session. And almost without fail, they do something interesting with their first line. Where do we get this instinct from? Well, we've probably picked up that's what great books do to get us hooked and keep us reading. We've already talked about the first line from George Orwell's *Nineteen Eighty-Four,* part of which is also the title of this section. Someone brought a book along to a session the other day with the fantastic first line:

I exist.

The thing is, while a great line can set the tone for a great novel (Orwell's clocks striking thirteen presage the unsettling, skewed reality that is the hallmark of *Nineteen Eighty-Four*), you could argue they're not that important. After all, if I've dug into my pocket to find nearly £10 to buy a book, or even if I've just gone to the effort of hopping on the bus to go to the library to pick out a book, then I've made something of a commitment to give this book a chance (at least once it makes its way off the very long waiting list on my bedside table of classic works of literature I've just not got round to yet – well, especially when *Doctor Who*'s on).

Most people, even the fussiest of readers, would give a book a chapter or two to establish its story or tone of voice before they decided to put it in the bin (or maybe give it to an unfortunate relative). You don't just read the first page, let alone the first line, and think to yourself, 'Hmmm, this is just *too* boring. It's back to the Jeffrey Archer for me.'

But we *are* that ruthless with business writing. How many times a week do you start reading a document someone has sent you – or worse, the e-mail to which they've attached their document – and decided that you've got plenty of other things that are worth wasting your time on first? In my case, it's a lot, and I think most people are pretty similar in this respect.

Heck, sometimes we don't even read the e-mail; we just read the subject line. If it's too dull, or too predictable, your reader is likely to either:

(a) bin it,

(b) file it, or

(c) pretend they're going to deal with it later until it slowly slips down into the fossil record of their inbox, proving that in e-mail, like life, it's survival of the fittest that holds sway.

So I think first lines (and titles) are more important in business writing than in fiction. And that's why it's such a missed opportunity to start with something flat. Too often our first lines are too long, rambling on with background or scene-setting or context or whatever we choose to call it, which is just going to make our reader switch off.

> first lines (and titles) are more important in business writing than in fiction

The answer, as so often in this book, is again to think like a journalist. As we've heard, to do the job of a journalist you have to accept that there's no way that every word you write will be read. So have a look at what they do to convince us. It's worth skipping past the first few pages of any day's newspaper, because as we've seen, that's usually where the stories are good enough to stand up in their own right. Look at what happens after that and you'll see first lines with shocking statements, strong opinions, quotations, alliteration and rhyme and all kinds of other stuff. Probably the most famous headline in the history of British newspaper journalism was one word. When British forces sank the Argentinian battleship the Belgrano during their war over the Falkland Islands, the *Sun* wrote:

GOTCHA

It was controversial, but controversy sells papers, because we like opinion. You won't always want to court controversy at the beginning of a piece of writing, but you will want to create an impact. Because if you don't do it then, you'll never do it.

A little while ago I was running a workshop and talking about the power of a surprising first line. One of the participants mentioned an Australian children's author called Paul Jennings. He said that his daughter loved the books of Paul Jennings so much that he'd inspired her to want to be a writer when she grew up. So his daughter had written to the author, asking for some advice on how to do it. And one bit of advice was about exactly this subject. He said 'Don't start your story, *I woke up, had a wash and brushed my teeth.* Start your story:

I did not eat your jeans.

Well, not on purpose anyway."

It's a great bit of advice. Of course, the most important aspect of it is doing something unexpected. But if you look at that opening – which presumably isn't even one he had ever actually used, just a writing example for keen young fans – there are at least another couple of interesting techniques he's using. His very first sentence is pretty short – six words – and the second even shorter. So that's a start with a lot of impact. And the word *Well* at the beginning of the sentence is crucial, too. It establishes a conversational tone, suggesting that there's a real person, with a real voice, narrating the story.

From background to foreground

The sort of writing that Paul Jennings is warning us about is the boring scene-setting. In the world of children's literature, that means don't do a list of really typical things any kid would do at the beginning of their day, because it's just too predictable. Again, exactly the same is true in business writing. I work with the British regulator for broadcasting and telecommunications, called Ofcom. They write big lengthy documents on serious subjects like 'regulation of the UK mobile phone industry', or 'the best date for switching off the UK analogue television signal'. One of the writers there put it brilliantly when he said that they have such a tendency towards scene-setting that their reports might as well start, 'In 1876, Alexander Graham Bell invented the telephone' for all the relevance much of this back story had to the issue at hand.

This scene-setting in business writing comes in different guises. Often it will be labelled *Background*. When a document starts with *Background*, it's always an alarm bell for me; after all, the clue is in the word. Why would you start with the background? You should be starting with the foreground – the most important or most interesting issue – because that's probably what's going to persuade me to read on. If you then manage to get me really interested in

> when a document starts with *Background*, it's always an alarm bell for me

the subject, I'll probably keep going and get to the background, but it's much less likely to happen the other way round.

It's not just the word *background*. Often the same material is lurking under different names. *Context*, for instance. I'm not saying that what you put in these sections can't be useful or relevant; of course it can. But it should just be somewhere else, not at that crucial moment in your story.

CHAPTER 14

Painting pictures

How to write for people who don't like reading

Why almost everything is the size of Wales

> **brilliant** tip
>
> Translate numbers and statistics into something more tangible.

Read the newspapers, or watch the news enough, in the UK and you'd be forgiven for thinking there are only two units of measurement for area. One is the size of Wales, and one is the size of a football pitch. Nearly every area you've ever heard described is one or the other, or a multiple of them. So 'Every year, an area three times the size of Wales is being deforested in Brazil.' Or, 'If all the unnecessary plastic bags we use in this country were collected together, they'd fill an area the size of a football pitch.' It's become a journalistic cliché, but it's still used the whole time. Why?

Well, it's because lots of us just aren't very good at getting our head around numbers and statistics. The actual number of hectares being deforested is virtually unintelligible, because I just don't have any real sense of what a hectare is (partly that's because I'm

> lots of us just aren't very good at getting our head around numbers and statistics

the child of a generation in limbo, taught metric measurements at school while the everyday currency of conversation is still about miles and stones and acres and leagues under the sea. So don't ask me how big an acre is, either). But if you get people to imagine something else instead, something of which they do have a vague notion of the size – like a sports field, or the area a country takes up on a map – they'll have a much better sense of the scale of what you're talking about. The same applies to whatever technical information you've got to communicate.

Recently we were working with a phone company that wanted to put on their customers' bills how much 'data' they could download as part of their tariff. Now, most of us simpletons don't even know what a data download really is, let alone what it means that I've got 5MB left this month. We recommended they translate this, even if it was only approximately, so that customers had a rough idea what they were banging on about. So they could say:

You've got 5MB left (that's roughly three songs you could download).

This trick of translating numbers into something more tangible (or at least imaginable) can also make statistics more personal. If you say ten per cent of the population is likely to die of a particular ailment (take your pick, there are many to choose from), it will have a certain impact on your reader. But if you say that one in ten people dies from it, it will have more impact. Suddenly we're not talking about numerical figures, but the figures of people we can imagine before our eyes. Of course, you could take this even further:

Think of ten people you know. Picture them, lined up in front of you. One of them is going to die.

Even more impact. This is the kind of tactic that charities use the whole time, because it takes a societal statistic and makes it much more of a personal issue. Yes, it's led to what some people call 'charity fatigue', where people begin to resent what they see as manipulation through this kind of message. But charities continue to use it because it's just more effective in their ultimate goal – getting money out of people.

Metaphors and similes

brilliant tip

Use written images to make your writing more emotional and immediate.

OK, here are two techniques that again might put us back in a boring old English lesson. They have fancy names, but actually they're things we do in conversation the whole time. We say that our journey to work was a *nightmare*; that someone we interviewed was a bit of a *cold fish*; that we're *dying* to go to the loo. Of course, none of that is literally true; you were not thrashing about and wailing on the bus in, nor was the woman in the interview scaly with eyes on the side of her head.

But using these techniques – essentially comparing something to something else with which it has some features in common – makes our writing more vivid. It also makes it more memorable; I've consistently found that people remember the metaphors I've used better than other things I've written. Just like the area the size of a football pitch, it's because you put a picture in their head, so they don't only have the words you used to go

> people remember the metaphors I've used better than other things I've written

on. Metaphors and similes can also allow you to bring in a bit of emotion to a piece of writing that otherwise might be a little flat.

It's something that newspaper journalists (them again) do all the time. The *Sun* for instance is full of metaphors. You'd never hear them talk about 'large petrochemical producer' BP; instead they'd call them an 'oil giant'. Again, BP is not literally a giant, lumbering round the countryside crushing farms in its wake, but a word like giant is a great way of getting across their size in a short word with a lot of power.

That's another thing about metaphor. Use it well, and it's a very efficient use of language; you manage to say a lot in few words, which after all is the aim of most business writing. The British motoring journalist Jeremy Clarkson has pretty much made a career out of metaphor. He arrived in a sphere that had always been pretty dull – people writing about engine capacity and cup holders – and transformed it. He transformed it into something so lively that he got people who weren't even interested in cars reading what he had to say. By comparing them to old ladies or German dogs he gets across the feel of what he's describing without getting too bogged down in the boring details. And it's served him well; he now gets to write columns ranting about other things, and his books are among the best selling in the UK.

> it's a very efficient use of language

Teaching an old dog new tricks

The effectiveness of metaphor was really brought home to me a while ago. The Liberal Democrats, the smallest of the big UK political parties, had just lost their leader, Sir Menzies Campbell, because he was fed up being told he was too old for the job. When he resigned, another fairly old chap called Vince Cable became temporary leader, while the party decided which of the young pups they wanted. Now, Vince Cable is an economist by training, and with his white hair and grey suits, he had a reputation for being a bit of a dullard.

His party were somewhat apprehensive, to say the least, about how he would do at Prime Minister's Questions, when he'd have to debate with Gordon Brown, who knows how to batter someone into submission with his words, even if he's not the quickest thinker in the world. But Vince took it by storm (there's a metaphor for you). He did so well, and so consistently, that some of his party started to wonder why on earth they weren't considering good old Vince for the post.

So what had he done? Well, I heard him interviewed on the radio and he said he'd been thinking about it in the bath. He was used to making speeches that gave him a relatively long time to build his argument, assemble his evidence and lead up to a conclusion. In this situation, he realised that he had to do something different. He recognised that whatever he said, it would probably be cut down to about ten seconds' worth of speech when it made it onto the evening news. What could you do in ten seconds?

He decided the best thing he could do was paint a picture in words. Paint the right picture, he thought, and it would resonate with people and stick with them, making the biggest possible use of his short little spot in the limelight. So that's what he did. In his first week, he said that:

> *The house has noticed the prime minister's remarkable transformation in the past few weeks – from Stalin to Mr Bean.*

The House of Commons fell about laughing. The news programmes, as Vince had predicted, picked up that line. And it was all over the papers the next day. Not bad for someone who'd been written off as a bit of a bore.

Using metaphor and simile is a creative technique. And the very thought of that will put some of you off, because you don't think of yourself as creative. Well, that's fine, because this isn't the sort of creativity where you have to sit in a field, waiting for

> you just think, OK,
> what can I compare
> that thing to?

inspiration to strike (although that sounds quite fun to me). The good news is that you can do this much more methodically if you like. You can say, right, here's the thing I've got to describe. That could be anything: a new product, a process you've got to explain, a person, your approach to something, whatever. Then you just think, OK, what can I compare that thing to? What if it were a...

Vehicle?

Building?

Animal?

Person doing a particular job?

Drink?

Piece of furniture?

Holiday?

Go through this list (and of course, add your own categories), and sooner or later you'll probably hit upon something that feels right. It's a technique that I used when I was writing the website for one of my clients a couple of years ago. They were a company that helped other companies design websites and other online gizmos. And they had an area of their own site which they were really excited about. They were excited about it because if you were one of the clients you could sign into this area, and, wait for it... look at their timesheets. I know! They thought it was fascinating, but it wasn't quite doing it for me. So, I asked them to explain what was so interesting. And they said, well, we charge for our work according to how much time we spend on things. But clients never believe us, and are always trying to negotiate down those costs. So, we needed a way to prove to them that we're telling the truth about who's working on things, and how long it's taking them.

Suddenly, it was starting to get more interesting. So this is the introduction I wrote to the page:

> *You know in posh restaurants you can look in the kitchen? This is our version (you can always nick a good idea).* Bon appétit.

Give your reader the right picture and it can make even the dullest thing that you're writing about seem engaging. Even timesheets, for goodness sake.

CHAPTER 15

More sound advice

How an unusual rhythm
will keep things interesting

Writing. Really. Short.

OK, we've already decided that stories are officially a Good Thing in writing. But of course, we don't always have the luxury of the space to let a tale unfurl, characters to develop or lessons to be learned. More and more I'm working with clients who have to write things in ridiculously small spaces; I don't just mean word limits – I mean things with *character* limits.

> we don't always have the luxury of the space to let a tale unfurl

Like what? Well, think of things like the tickertapes at the top of websites, or the text that scrolls across the screen of digital radio sets; marketing in the form of text message, when one letter over the limit will cost you twice as much (and probably mean your reader doesn't read it). Even tools like Instant Messenger, which some of my clients are already using with the same relish that the rest of us save for e-mail.

How do you make an impact, and get your point across, in a situation like that, while not reducing what you've got to say to the cold, hard, factual style of a telegram? Well, a little while ago I was reading in the *Guardian* an article about the best story Ernest Hemingway felt he'd ever written. And that story was just six words long:

For sale: baby shoes. Never worn.

It is brilliant. For most people, it packs quite an emotional punch, despite its length (although some people also say, 'What's the big deal? They were just the wrong colour'). So the *Guardian* decided to ask a number of contemporary authors to write a six-word story of their own. Here are some of my favourites:

'It can't be. I'm a virgin.'
Kate Atkinson

See that shadow? (It's not yours.)
Jim Crace

Dad called: DNA back: he isn't.
Helen Fielding

Evil isn't necessarily unkind. Gran next.
DBC Pierre

Thought love must fade: but no.
George Saunders

(If you're hungry for more of these, a book has been published called *Not Quite What I Was Planning*, a collection of life stories in six words by people famous and people not-so.)

Whichever ones appeal most to you, it's amazing that these authors manage to get a real sense of their tone of voice across, despite the squeeze of words. If you've read *Vernon God Little* by DBC Pierre, you'll recognise the dark humour and barely hidden menace in his six words; likewise Helen Fielding's breezy take on human relationships. They manage to provoke different reactions – fear, inspiration, embarrassment – and even, if you read Kate Atkinson's story this way, sum up the annunciation of the Virgin Mary's unplanned pregnancy. If you can do this in six words, then writing a headline shouldn't be all that difficult after all.

*!?$

It's worth looking at one of the tricks the authors are pulling to get their short-story form to work. Look at them as a set, and you'll notice that not one of them has written a straight six-word sentence. The most obvious aspect of this is that there's a lot of punctuation going on, helping to break these lines up into smaller elements; stories with a beginning, middle and end, or question and answer, or set-up and punchline.

They've realised that to inject the energy, or drama, or intrigue, into something so short, you need to play around with the sentence structure. I've said punctuation was invented for actors, to tell them what to do when they're performing (a full stop is a big pause; a comma less so). Think like an actor, and it's clear here that they'd be working quite hard, even with only six words to play with.

So, now you're up for the challenge, let's get even tougher. Often in workshops, we ask people to write haikus. A haiku is a Japanese poem, with a very strict structure:

> you need to play around with the sentence structure

three lines, seventeen syllables in total, split between the lines (five in the first line; seven in the next; five in the final one).

If you scour the internet, you'll find hundreds of haiku sites in Japanese, naturally. But there are also a ton of them in English, too. There's something about the form that tickles people's fancy; it's just enough room to say something, but too short for you to say it in an ordinary or expected way.

While you're surfing, you'll probably find a website devoted to the error message haikus. They imagine that instead of the typical Microsoft-style message you'd usually get on your computer ('Due to error 479 everything you were working on last night has gone away forever. Loser'), you'd get instead a haiku, communicating not just the information, but something about the world, philosophy and life, at the same time. Here are three of my favourites:

> *Yesterday it worked.*
> *Today it is not working;*
> *Windows is like that.*

> *A crash reduces*
> *Your expensive computer*
> *To a simple stone.*

> *Three things are certain:*
> *Death, taxes and lost data.*
> *Guess which has occurred.*

I think they'd make you feel a little better disposed towards Bill Gates and Microsoft than the usual, don't you?

---

brilliant action

Try writing a haiku; it's tougher than it seems. Try answering the question 'what do I do?' in a haiku (answer it for you, not for me, obviously). You'll find that once again, you're forced to do unusual things with your sentence structure, which will make what you're saying much more intriguing than your usual version.

The syllable limit in a haiku also has another handy benefit; suddenly, those big long corporate words become very expensive. Heck, use a phrase like *operational efficiency*, and you'll suddenly discover that half of your haiku has been used up before you've even said anything. You'll need to say what you've got to say in much simpler, or more unusual, terms.

You can use these techniques to bring to life a really dull bit of really short writing. But they'll even help you out if you're doing a longer, more typical piece of writing. I use these techniques when I'm writing, and suddenly I realise, in the middle of paragraph three or something, that even I have lost the thread of what I'm saying (and of course, if I've lost the thread, there's not much hope for my readers). Sometimes, I'll put what I'm writing to one side and have a go at writing it either as a six-word story, or as a haiku.

> use these techniques to bring to life a really dull bit of really short writing

It does two things. First, it forces me to *really* get to the point of what I've got to say. But it also helps me put it in simple, interesting terms. Now, of course, I might never end up using that actual wording – after all, even I have to admit that there will be some forms of serious business writing where a tiny Japanese poem really isn't going to come over that well. But usually I can take something from that wording: a word itself; a rhythm or structure; an idea or an image. Then just plugging that element into the main thing that I'm writing – or even better, into its title or headline – will usually add a bit of spice, and bring it to life.

The power of a single word

 **tip**

Single-word sentences have a big, surprising impact.

Ready?

Every now and again, write a one-word sentence. One. See? Unusual, isn't it?

The odd one-word sentence is really useful to make your writing less predictable. It changes the rhythm, and adds a bit of drama, or emphasis. Really. At the beginning of a paragraph, it'll set you off on a different tack to the way you'd usually start, and help change the shape and feel of the rest of what you're writing.

So, when I've had clients getting me to write about things that I'm not particularly interested in (financial services spring to mind, pensions especially), I have to keep myself amused and engaged by using tricks like that.

Pensions. I'd start like that, and it sends you off in a particular direction. Something like:

Pensions. We all have to have them but none of us wants to think about them.

...and already I'm off in a direction that's not the most obvious, and therefore more interesting. But start with a really random word and it can really bring your writing to life.

Spanner. Unhelpful when it's in the works, a nice surprise at the beginning of a paragraph (that's how you do it, you see?). In fact, you can set yourself the challenge of starting with ever more outlandish words, trying somehow to make them work, and seeing what they do to your writing. Typically they force you to do something a little bit off the beaten track. And that kind of writing risk nearly always pays a dividend.

> set yourself the challenge of starting with ever more outlandish words

Repetition, repetition, repetition

 brilliant tip

Use repetition to reinforce a point or make an idea more memorable.

Back to the things we were told not to do at school. This time, 'Don't repeat words.' And, often, that's good advice. I've frequently had people read out bits of their own writing in my own workshops and suddenly they realise they've used some bit of business flummery (most of the time it's the usual suspects – *appropriate*, *strategic*, *effective* and the like) ten times in one paragraph, and not surprisingly, it sounds daft.

But that's when people are repeating things in an unplanned way; when the same word has got stuck in our head and we can't think of anything else decent to write. But when you're repeating something deliberately, for effect, it can be quite powerful. It works, because it lodges an idea in your head. Some of the oldie readers will remember a singer called Joan

> it lodges an idea in your head

Armatrading (who deserves to be famous just for her name alone, frankly). One of the real features of her lyrics is her repetition of the same words over and over again. Take the song 'I'm Lucky':

I'm lucky
I'm lucky
I can walk under ladders
Yes I'm so lucky
That I'm as lucky
As me

Get the point? That's right: she's lucky. Or her biggest hit, 'Love and Affection':

With a friend
I can smile...
But with a lover
I could really move
Really move
I could really dance
Really dance
Really dance
Really dance
I could really move
Really move
Really move
Really move

It looks a little bit ridiculous when you write it out like that, but trust me, in the song, it works. I once saw her interviewed on the telly about why she did it, and she said something like, 'Well, I want to make sure the listener gets the point.' And she's right; say it enough, and you remember it. Again, it's something we do naturally in conversation. Try talking to someone about something you're really interested in, or really passionate about, without using the magic words 'really, really...'. It's, er, really difficult. And you'll find yourself doing things like that over and over again (see).

Now, in your piece of crucial business writing, you're probably not going to do a Joan Armatrading-style repetition of the same line six times. But you can use the same technique. One of the most famous advertising straplines in the UK over the last ten years has been: 'The future's bright. The future's Orange.' The repetition, alongside the twist at the end of the second sentence, is what makes it memorable. And of course, it's a trick that politicians use all the

> it's a trick that politicians use all the time

time; ask many people in the UK what was Tony Blair's main policy when he won his landslide election victory in 1997 and many of them will still remember 'education, education, education' (even though it's not really a policy in itself). Or 'Tough on crime, tough on the causes of crime' (which pulls exactly the same trick as the Orange line). Or think back to Churchill:

> *We shall fight on the beaches, we shall fight on the landing grounds, we shall fight in the fields and in the streets, we shall fight in the hills; we shall never surrender.*

It feels a bit cheap to analyse something as powerful and important as that speech, but I'm sure he did. He knew what would make his words emphatic, powerful, compelling. This example is from a speech, designed to be read out – performed, in fact. But your reader will be hearing your words in their head, even if they're not reading them out loud. That's why the very best business writing – often advertising – works really well when it's read out, even if it was never intended for that.

In workshops I often show people an example which is a particular favourite of mine. It was an ad for the charity VSO, Voluntary Service Overseas, trying to persuade people to pack in their jobs and go and volunteer in a developing country. A big ask, a football commentator would say about that. The ad appeared on trains, buses and tubes and the like; situations when you had a bit of time to read it, and to give it time to build to a crescendo. It starts by describing most people's day at work:

predictable, trivial, mundane. And then it contrasts that with what it would be like if you went to help other people, and make a difference to the world. Powerful, emotional subject matter to start with. But it ends with a great flurry of repetition:

> *This is your chance. This is the ad. This is the number... This is the website... This is the day.*

People who've been schooled in marketing will tell you every ad like this needs a 'call to action' – something telling you what to do now – usually something naff like 'Ring this number TODAY to see how you can take part.' The VSO ad doesn't need it. The repetition is all you need to convince you. Of course, it wouldn't work on everyone, and indeed they've got a clear idea who their target audience is (after all, does the developing world really need a business writing trainer?). A few times I've shown the ad to groups of social workers I've been working with. Usually by the time we get to these final five lines, they're all desperately scrabbling round in their bags to find a pen and paper so they can write down the details and send off their applications. If you're the sort of person who might be tempted, it's amazing how a little linguistic trick like repetition can be the thing that gives you the motivation to do something different.

A little alliteration

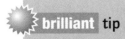 **tip**

Repeat the same sounds to make your writing more memorable.

While we're trying to lodge things in people's heads, it's probably time to talk about alliteration. That's probably a word you last heard at school, so even now you may be running for the hills. Alliteration just means repeating the same sound (technically, a consonant, but we don't need to worry about that here. Life's too short). It's what makes tongue-twisters difficult:

Peter Piper picked a peck of pickled peppers.

There are two bits of alliteration going on there, with the *p* and *ck* sounds. Switching between the two is pretty hard for our simple mouths. But with just one sound, repeated, but not too much, it gives what you're writing a bit of rhythm and a bit of punch. So, instead of writing:

> it gives what you're writing a bit of rhythm and a bit of punch

Remuneration should acknowledge how well people have met their objectives

you could write:

Pay people for how well they perform.

Again, you might think it's weird to suggest using what is essentially a poetic technique in a serious, business document. But I only suggest it because it works; it really does help you get your point lodged in your readers' minds. So much so that it's a trick that's been used in even the most serious of situations. Shortly after London was bombed by terrorists in July 2005, police raided various houses in the city of Leeds, looking for suspects and clues. But, of course, they knew that it could be quite scary for the local residents to think potential terrorists were living among them. So the police took to the airwaves and kept saying that they wanted the local community to be:

Alert but not alarmed.

They repeated this phrase again and again: alert but not alarmed. Alert but not alarmed. It struck me as amazing – but also completely logical – that at a time of national crisis police were using the repetition of sounds to make sure what they said was remembered, and hit home (see, another bit there).

CHAPTER 16

Screenwriting

Or how to write for a teeny
bit of space

wrote most of this book a couple of years ago (though luckily *Doctor Who*'s still on the telly, and Belle & Sebastian are still making records, so I don't have to go through changing all the cultural references to sound up-to-date). But since I did, one thing about business writing has, if not transformed, then exploded even further. And that's writing for digital media.

Now, writing for websites and e-mail has been going on for a good decade. But there's loads of what we write now that our readers never, ever, see on a bit of paper. Heck, they might not even get to see it on a very big screen; because these days we're reading many of our e-mails on the little screens of iPhones, BlackBerrys and other smartphones; we're sending our customers text messages; or, we're writing things like tweets where even if you see them on quite a big screen, there's still a character limit to stop you blethering on.

So how do you write for these digital media? Well, there's a lot of kidology that goes on from people passing themselves off as 'web writers' who suggest that us mere mortals should never even think of trying to write anything online. That there's a whole set of skills you need to learn from years of practice. That's bunkum. The good news is that if you apply the techniques I've been talking about in this book, you'll be well on your way. There's nothing fundamentally different about the skills you need to write digital stuff; you just need to be even more ruthless about applying them. At The Writer, we often say that web writing is like normal

> there's nothing fundamentally different about the skills you need to write digital stuff

writing, only more so. Sure, there's the odd specific thing that's worth knowing (and we'll get onto those in a tick), but by and large, what readers want is the same: for you to get to the point, quick; to skip the bits they're not bothered about; and for you to sound at least normal, and, even better, interesting.

Over the next few pages, then, we'll look at those few tricks that you just need to add into your linguistic kitbag to make sure you're fully prepared for a digital adventure.

Writing web pages

Remember those *Choose Your Own Adventure* books we had when we were little? 'If you stay to fight the dragon, turn to Chapter 4; if you run away to get a fire extinguisher, turn to Chapter 17.' They were pretty clever, because each bit had to make sense in its own right, but also had to be able to deal with people coming to it and leaving from it in a few different ways.

Well, that's how most websites work, too. Your pages might be part of a big, overall structure, and you can have a go at leading people through it the way you'd

> start with the most important thing that page is about

like, but there'll be people who just land on one random page (maybe thanks to Google), and that one random page still needs to make sense to them.

Less is more

There's an important physiological thing that shapes web writing: it's actually more tiring to read on screen (about 25% more tiring, apparently). That means we read more slowly. Which means we have even less tolerance for waffle than we do on paper. So cut down the amount of text, cut out the salesy adjectives, and use lots of sub-headings to help your reader skim-read, even if your paragraphs are only a couple of lines long.

brilliant tip

Natural language makes your page easier to search (and find).

A big thing to bear in mind is how your reader has found your web page. Not many of them will have studiously typed in your URL, got to your homepage and patiently clicked through your well-thought-out structure. Most of them will have Googled it, and whoomph, there they are.

So an obvious question then is: what are they Googling? (Other search engines are available.) The important point is that people don't search for what you call things, they search for what they call them, so they'll search 'cashing in a policy' not 'policy surrender'. Different search engines work in different ways (and Google are so clever – and paranoid – that they change their search methodology every now and again to make sure it doesn't get too easy to second-guess), but most of them prioritise headings, links and first paragraphs. That means that if there are important words your would-be readers are going to search, that's the place to put them.

Despite their best efforts, a whole industry has grown up around second-guessing Google, called SEO, or search engine optimisation. These people will get your website to the top of Google for a week, but also make it sound rubbish in the process. The worst SEO types will tell you that if you're selling fire exit signs, the phrase to mention lots is, naturally enough, 'fire exit signs'. The more you say it, the more likely you are to reach the exalted top of Google's rankings. The trouble is, they want you to write your website so it sounds like this:

We sell fire exit signs

If you want to buy a fire exit sign, you've come to the right place, because we sell fire exit signs. Fire exit signs are the heart of our business. We don't think you'll find any better fire exit signs in the whole of Christendom, because that's what we do, really: fire exit signs.

Now, much as Google might love this, most readers won't. (And of course, if you do more than just fire exit signs, this gets harder and harder to write without sounding bonkers). So you need to find a balance between something that's practical and something that's still engaging.

brilliant tip

Use links that explain what happens if you follow them.

A good thing to do if you're writing web pages is to think about some of your potential readers for whom it mightn't be so easy. For instance, people who are blind or visually impaired in some way have clever gizmos that can read out web text. These gizmos, called screen readers, will read out all the links on a page, so that blind readers can quickly get to the thing they're after. That would be great, but on many websites, if you just read out the links, you get this:

Click here

Click here

Click here

That's because they're part of sentences like *To see how to get a parking permit, click here.* Obviously not much use if all you hear is the linky bit. So make your links explain what you get when you click the link. Try something like this: *Find out how to get a parking permit.*

No dumping

A great thing about the internet is just how much information you can find. The flipside of that is it can sometimes be buried in acres of text or huge, sprawling PDFs you need to download. So don't use your website as a dumping ground for gigantic reference documents. Or if you do, summarise the main points on a web page, so your reader doesn't

> don't use your website as a dumping ground

have to do all the work. Remember that most people have gone to your website (rather than, say, sent off for your annual report) because they want the quick and easy version.

The same goes for the text itself on web pages. Too often people take text they've written for other media, like articles and brochures, bung the same words up on their website or intranet and think they've done their job. Wrong. Think about how much more slowly we read online; anything you put on the web needs to be short and easy to skim. If your original isn't, it'll be even worse online.

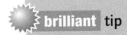 **brilliant** tip

Web copy can go down as well as up.

A brilliant thing about the internet is how easy it is to get topical information out into the world – quickly. So it's a brilliant place for publicising events, competitions, and that kind of stuff. Just be careful that, if you're running a website, you take things down as well as up. What was topical last week looks old hat this. Go to a website that's going on about things that happened a month ago, or three months ago, and it seems like nothing's happened since. Your reader starts thinking, has the business gone under? Maybe the owner's in prison? Often no news is better than old news.

Writing e-mails for little screens

I'm one of those people who's lucky enough not to be in the office very much (lovely though the people in my office are). Which means I spend much of my life reading e-mails on the tiny screens of little phoney things. Most of the time, it's a brilliant convenience; sometimes it's a bloody nuisance. And boy, does it sort the writing men from the boys (or sheep from the goats, or wheat from the chaff; pick the metaphor that most appeals). The best e-mails are short, sharp, easy.

> The best e-mails are short, sharp, easy

The worst are rambling monsters that trigger repetitive strain injury in my scrolling finger before I even know what they're about. So you need to rigorously apply two rules from way back at the beginning when we talked about structure.

Remember the inverted pyramid?

So, start with your most important thing. In an e-mail, that's often the bit we're used to putting at the end: your conclusion, or a question, or a list of actions for someone. If you're feeling really generous, you might tell them right upfront if they need to do anything about your e-mail, or if it's just for their information (but remember, if it's just for information, many readers will switch off at that point).

If you've got a lot of things to cover in one e-mail, and that scrolling finger is going to be working overtime, tell them upfront what's coming up with a mini-list of contents, and use sub-headings in the same words. That way, they'll be able to skip merrily to the bit they care about.

 brilliant tip

Watch out for too many links or wacky formatting

You need to be a wee bit careful if you know someone's going to be reading something while they're on the move. Things that look whizzy and neat in an e-mail on your computer screen can turn into monstrosities of gobbledygook on an iPhone or BlackBerry.

So watch out for hyperlinks (the link will appear, but perhaps as the full, two-line URL, not the neat little embedded, underlined word you put in your e-mail). And things like smileys are always getting mangled into something funny looking (often a capital J on my iPhone; no idea why). Even though I've learnt that capital J is someone's attempt at a nod or a wink, it still befuddles me temporarily (and I don't know whether they're nodding or winking, which can get you into all kinds of hot water). All of which is just another good reason hardly ever to use smileys (if you thought I got stroppy about exclamation marks, you should see me when I get smiley-strewn e-mails). The trick is to get whatever it is you want to express into your writing, rather than relying on an emoticon to make you seem human.

Writing blogs

Who isn't writing a blog these days? Well, me, because a few people have given me whole books to sound off in.

And that idea of 'sounding off' is important. Even when businesses write blogs, they're not great places for spouting the corporate line (especially if you leave the comments open). Part of the point of a blog is that it's informal and personal. On a blog we want to see something 'real' of the writer – their opinions, their sense of humour, a bit of honesty or self-deprecation.

Businesses who allow their blog writers to do that do well, especially if the blog is being written by one of the high-ups like a CEO. But if it doesn't sound authentic, be prepared for a roasting. Most readers can spot if a blog is being spun, or even ghost-written.

So the moral of the story is to only do a blog if you're willing to be open and honest, and to take the rough with the smooth. And if you're not, just don't do one. As blogs proliferate, few people have time to read that many anyway, so your daily-updated diary about the goings on in your gearbox factory might not get *that* many readers in any event.

> only do a blog if you're willing to be open and honest

And it also means that blogs usually work best if they're attributed to a particular person. Yes, that person might be representing the company, and probably isn't writing what they would on their own personal blog. But knowing there's an individual behind that bit of writing makes us much more open to what they've got to say, and allows the writer a bit more leeway to put in some of their own personality, and make it more engaging as a result.

Writing texts

Getting a text right is a difficult job. There's often a character limit (usually 140), including spaces, so you've got to be pretty succinct in what you say. On the other hand, if you're a multi-national company sending service updates to your customers, you probably don't want to abbreviate things so much that you sound like you're trying to be down with the kidz.

So use your nous about your audience; I don't think I've ever written anything for a client that involved a 'u' (instead of *you)* or *We're coming to fix the boiler. C U l8r.* But *can't* and *won't* and all that malarkey is great: it'll make you sound natural and save you some characters here and there.

And think back to the six-word stories. Don't write everything as one sentence, however much you might feel you've got to squeeze in. Break your sentences up. Try a really short one. Ask a question or two. It'll cost you a few characters' worth of punctuation, but it'll be well worth it for the pace and rhythm.

Writing tweets

I have to confess that I'm not on Twitter. I get distracted enough in my working life; if I was tweeting too I'd probably never get anything done. So I need to tip my hat to my colleague Nick Padmore for these tips. He's The Writer's Twitterer-in-chief. (Incidentally, we ran a little Twitter competition to come up with best new past tense of 'to tweet'. Our favourite was 'twote': 'Oh, I already twote about that yesterday.' I love it. Anyway.)

Naturally, much of what we've said about blogs and texts holds true: keep the structure and rhythm of what you've got to say interesting, and don't get all corporate. But there are a couple of other things to think about too.

What I'm about to say goes against the whole spirit of Twitter, which is kind of communal, and supportive and a little bit hippy, but as a writer, Twitter is pretty competitive. Your words appear in a big stream alongside other people's, and it's up to you to get people to follow the links you recommend, or get people to re-tweet your words of wisdom in the face of that competition.

So it means you need to work pretty hard to intrigue people in the few words you've got; no use just slapping up a link and keeping your fingers crossed; you need to seduce them, or provoke them, or intrigue them.

brilliant tip

Tweet enough, but not too much.

Like with your website, you need to keep on it with Twitter. One Tweet every few months is not really going to build you any kind of following (or help people get to know you, which is part of the point). Equally if you're tweeting every five minutes with what type of sandwich people are having in the office, it's going to get pretty annoying. A few good'uns a day seems to be about the right limit.

you need to keep on it with Twitter

There's other, slightly more technical detail about hashtags and square brackets, but I'll leave that to the real geeks. Who knows if we'll be writing on Twitter in another couple of years (remember *Friends Reunited*, anyone?), but for now, that's the way to do it.

CHAPTER 17

And finally...

How a fresh look at the
order of what you're writing
can make a difference

little tip if you feel like your writing isn't working, even after all this stuff, and particularly if it seems to be taking a long time to get to the point, is to take a fresh look at the order of what you're writing. Right back at the beginning of this book, I was talking about this order of things in your writing. Sometimes, when you get to the end of it all, and you still feel your writing's a bit flat, it might be that a final tweak of the order is all you need.

Try changing the order of what you've written, while keeping the words pretty much the same. You can do this within paragraphs, or across the whole piece if you prefer. If you're not sure where to start, try changing your third sentence so it becomes your first one (you'll probably have to do a wee bit of rewriting to make it work). But this is as close as you'll get to writing magic. Swap the order like that, and most writing mysteriously comes to life.

> this is as close as you'll get to writing magic

I think it's because often we take a little while to get going. It's like doing the long jump; we start off with a hop and a skip to get our ear in and get a little rhythm going before we finally launch off into the big jump. But when you're watching the long jump, it's obviously not the run-up we're all interested in, it's the jump. The same is true in your writing; your reader is hoping you'll start with a leap: something bold, surprising or intriguing. It's much more interesting to start there and then work backwards to make the leap make sense.

And one final thing to bear in mind: if you're changing the order of paragraphs, it probably means you'll be going for a slightly unorthodox structure. That means, as we've seen before, you just need to add some sub-headings so that your reader can see what direction you're going in.

PART 5

The end

CHAPTER 18

It ain't over till it's over

Or what you need to do before the writing goes out the door

Well, that's not quite it. Let's say you've produced a great piece of writing (by now, I've got faith in you). It's clear, well structured, succinct and enlivened with a smattering of magic. Your final job is to make sure that you're not so wrapped up in perfecting your writing that you've missed something blindingly obvious which is going to trip your reader up, or worse, think you're a stylish bluffer prone to silly mistakes. It's time for a final edit, and some proof-reading.

The longer you can leave it between finishing writing and doing all of this stuff, the better; the more distance you have, the more objective you'll be about your writing, and the easier you'll find it to spot, and be honest about, its strengths and weaknesses. At the very least, leave something overnight if you can. A new day will give you a new pair of eyes.

And while your biggest edit might be at the end, it really can (and should) be happening all the way through the writing process. Because editing is really just stepping back and thinking. It's about asking yourself:

> editing is really just stepping back and thinking

Do I really need to make that point?

Will my reader understand that?

Is that in the right place?

Behind many a great writer is a brilliant editor, and most good business writers also need to be good editors of their own work. But because distance is important, it might just be that you'll always be a wee bit too close to your own writing to see the good from the bad. In which case, maybe you shouldn't be editing your own work at all.

Seeing other people

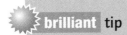 **tip**

Get other people to read your writing.

When you've finished your bit of writing, and you've done the best edit of your own writing that you can, ask someone else. However good a writer you are, we can all benefit from another point of view. It helps for a number of reasons:

we can all benefit from another point of view

1 **They might be more realistic** about what a reader really is interested in, and more honest about when you're just blethering on about something that only you care about.

2 **They'll see or hear things that you don't**. When you're very close to your own writing, you stop reading it; instead you read what you *think* you wrote, or what you intended to write. A reader with a fresh pair of eyes and ears will be responding to what's actually there on the page.

3 **They'll give you good ideas**. Most of us see writing as quite a solitary activity; that's why the stereotype of a writer is of someone sat on their own in an attic room agonising over

apostrophes. Interestingly, this slightly romantic stereotype exists even of business writers, who you would hope are a little better connected to the real world – so they can write about it – and who you'd imagine should be spending quite a lot of time with other people – like the clients who are giving them their work, for example. But it doesn't have to be lonely. Let your colleague-cum-editor make some suggestions, too.

Unfortunately though, there will be some times when you are just completely left to your own devices. So what do you do then?

More proof of the pudding

brilliant tip

Reading out will help you proof-read. Or, put a dot over every word as you read.

The final check is the proof-read. That's to make absolutely sure that you've not spelt a word wrong, missed out a crucial word or made any other kind of terrible typographic error which is going to distract your reader from the brilliance of your thinking, and instead make you sound like a dimwit.

Now, I am not the person to lecture anyone on proof-reading; I'm terrible at it. And like anyone, I'm particularly terrible at it when it comes to my own writing. I will do anything to get someone else to proof-read what I've done – offering to do the same for them, or swapping proof-reading for lunch. But I have to admit that *I'm* not even very good at it when it comes to someone else's writing – I just don't have the eye for detail. This is something that's very confusing for my clients, because that's exactly what they expect a writer to be able to do: spell the words right that they can't, and get the grammar right that they don't.

But there are proof-reading techniques that you can use to help you out (and even a system of crazy symbols all of its own, if you really want to go the whole hog). When one of our clients asked for a proof-reading course, we asked one of our best and favourite proof-readers what she'd propose. She came up with three days of the theory and practice. Now, I'm all for doing things thoroughly. But which of us really has three days to devote to becoming better at spotting where a hyphen should be an en rule? (Exactly. Most normal people don't even know what an en rule is! Or need to.) Crikey, *Lord of the Rings* was long enough.

> there are proof-reading techniques that you can use to help you out

First, as I keep saying, read it out. That will put you in a slightly different mode, and help you spot mistakes you wouldn't otherwise. If you really can't read it out (I don't know, let's say you've been locked in the British Library against your will), then here's a trick a colleague taught me. With the text in front of you, read it in your head, and when you've read each word, put a dot on the top of each one. This approach really slows you down, so you have to be sure you've read what the word actually says, and means you can't invent a word that isn't really there but should be. It's still not foolproof. If you're me, typos try *really* hard to inveigle their way into my writing. But it'll get you a long way down the road to perfection.

Does it really matter?

Of course, there are some people who'd argue that this stuff isn't important. Make your content interesting, get the rhythm right, and make it memorable enough and grammar, punctuation and the like are just pedestrian pedantry. And you know what? I'm pretty sympathetic to that view. But sticking to the spirit of being pessimistic about your readers, there is a whole load of them out there (maybe you're one of them, dear reader) who are bothered by this stuff, and who just might stop taking you seriously if you look either like you don't know some of these rules, or maybe don't care about them. We've all heard people say that if you have these kinds of mistake on your CV, you might never get an interview, and I've seen it happen several times.

But at The Writer we've also given a job to someone (a wannabe writer, mark you) who got their application in late, had typos all over their CV, and called the person they were e-mailing it to Beth instead of Donna. But you'd have to be:

(a) pretty talented, and

(b) a pretty nice person, or

(c) maybe just pretty

to get away with that. Is that a risk you really want to run?

And of course this whole section is really nothing more than a long apology note. Nearly all books end up with a typo in them somewhere. As I tap this draft cackhandedly into my laptop, I'm sure it's riddled with them. But if they get through to the final print, it's not my fault.

It's not my job.

CHAPTER 19

The end is nigh

So, ladies and gentlemen, that really is it. Almost everything I know about writing. Hopefully at least some of what I've said has stuck in your head, or hit home, or got you thinking in a different way. On first reading, it's unlikely that you'll have taken everything in (after all, it's been a list of more than three things), but keep this on your desk and on a slow day you'll be able to dip in for a linguistic top-up.

dip in for a linguistic top-up

But because I'm a pessimist about my readers (yes, even you) and because I know just how many people skip to the back of whodunnits to find out, well, whodunnit, before returning to the beginning and congratulating themselves on knowing that they would've worked it out, here's the whole damned book in twelve easy steps. Take it, pin it to your wall, and live by it. But if you're going for that promotion, don't tell your friends.

brilliant checklist

1   **Decide on your content**. Write down every point you could potentially make.

2   **Be ruthless**. Question whether you really need all of it. Cut anything that's not really important. Ask yourself: would it matter if someone had to ring me up for that extra bit of information? Remember, the more you write, the fewer people are reading.

3 **Get the order right**. This doesn't have to be the most logical order. Remember, more people are reading at the beginning, so that's where you should be making your crucial points. Write the summary first if it helps. Don't start with background.

4 **Pick a theme...** if you think it'll make your writing more interesting, or help your material hang together.

5 **Include contents...** if what you're writing is long or complicated or detailed enough to warrant it.

6 **Include sub-headings**. It's your job to make it easy to skim-read. Use sub-headings that are helpful or interesting, not just the usual *Introduction* and *Conclusions*.

7 **Make a good start**. Make sure your first line, or title, is interesting enough for your reader to keep reading.

8 **Write like you speak**. It doesn't have to be slangy, but write it as you'd say it to your reader in person. Avoid jargon and corporatespeak.

9 **Mix it up**. Vary the length and style of your sentences to keep your reader engaged.

10 **Make it memorable**. Use rhythm, rhyme, repetition, alliteration, metaphor – anything, really, that will stop your writing feeling like the same old same old.

11 **Read it out**. Check how it sounds by reading it out. Change anything that doesn't sound natural.

12 **Get someone else to proof-read it**. Or if you have to do it yourself, pretend to be someone else.

And Bob's your uncle, to end on a cliché. And by now you should have a much more interesting way to end than that. If you have, nip over to Kennington and maybe you could let me know. But not while *Doctor Who's* on, obviously.

the brilliant series

Fast and engaging, the *Brilliant* series works hard to make sure you stand out from the crowd. Each *Brilliant* book has been carefully crafted to ensure everything you read is practical and applicable – to help you make a difference now.

9780273722328

9780273720591

9780273717355

9780273743217

9780273726463

9780273725114

9780273721239

9780273712350

9780273734147

9780273714804

9780273730675

9780273730910